Vintage Paintings of Children
Another Grayscale Coloring Book
Volume 1.
Copyright 2020, Lynn Thomas. All Rights Reserved.

Dedicated to my Great Grandmother Malone, who had the great taste to decorate our family home with prints of gorgeous paintings from the Great Masters, and instilled in me as a child, an appreciation for beautiful, classical art.

****

This book may not be reproduced in any form, in whole or in part, or stored or transmitted by any means, known now or by something developed in the future. The designs in this book are for your personal use only and may be reproduced by the purchaser for that use.

You are free to share your finished colored pages as long as credit is given to the artist. No uncolored pages are to be shared or posted online.

All other uses, especially commercial use, are strictly forbidden without written permission by the creator, Lynn Thomas.

Copyright Lynn Thomas 2020 All Rights Reserved

****

This book is the result of painstaking research. I scoured the inter webs for classical paintings of children that were in the public domain. And I ended up with a treasure trove of wonderful paintings I'd never seen before. The list of the paintings is at the end of the book. Each painting has been transformed into a details grayscale image, lightened and sharpened so that when you color it, there isn't much gray to be seen.

Each grayscale image is like the sketch for the beginning of your work of art. That's how I look at grayscale coloring: the Artist provides you with the sketch for your painting, and you chose how to fill the rest in. Part of the beauty of grayscale coloring is that no two colored images look alike; it is your personal color choices, and your personal execution and interpretation, yours alone!

There are many youtube videos available for you to learn how to do grayscale coloring. If you are challenged, and do not understand how to go about it, go to youtube and search for what your issue is, and you're sure to find some excellent tutorials.

And, allow me to personally invite you to join my facebook group "Creative Studio Designs."

https://www.facebook.com/groups/384294649651299

We're building a group of Grayscale Colorists who appreciate high quality images. Once there, I welcome your feedback on the kinds of books you'd like to see from me in the future. And if you have questions, please ask them, we have a wonderful community of colorists of all skill levels and a wide variety of experience, who will encourage you, and help you along your journey.

And, if you prefer to print out your own images on your own paper, you can obtain copies of my books in pdf form on Etsy. My shop is also titled "Creative Studio Designs."

Here is the link to my Etsy Shop:

https://www.etsy.com/ shop/CreativeStudDesigns

My hope is that my books will provide you many hours of creative coloring and soul nurturing moments, and give you beautiful art as a result.

My best to you, and I hope I get to see your colored images!

Lynn Thomas

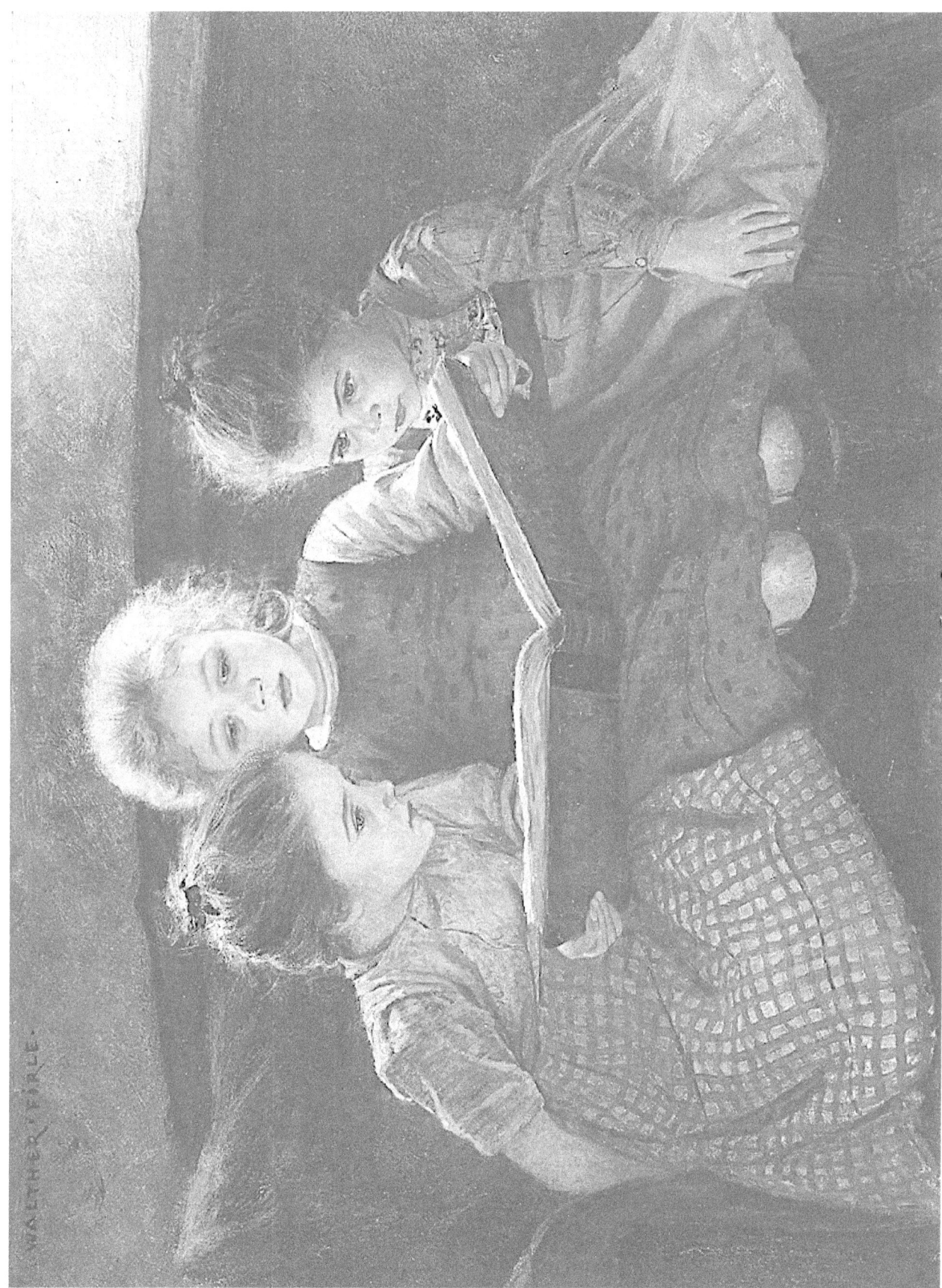

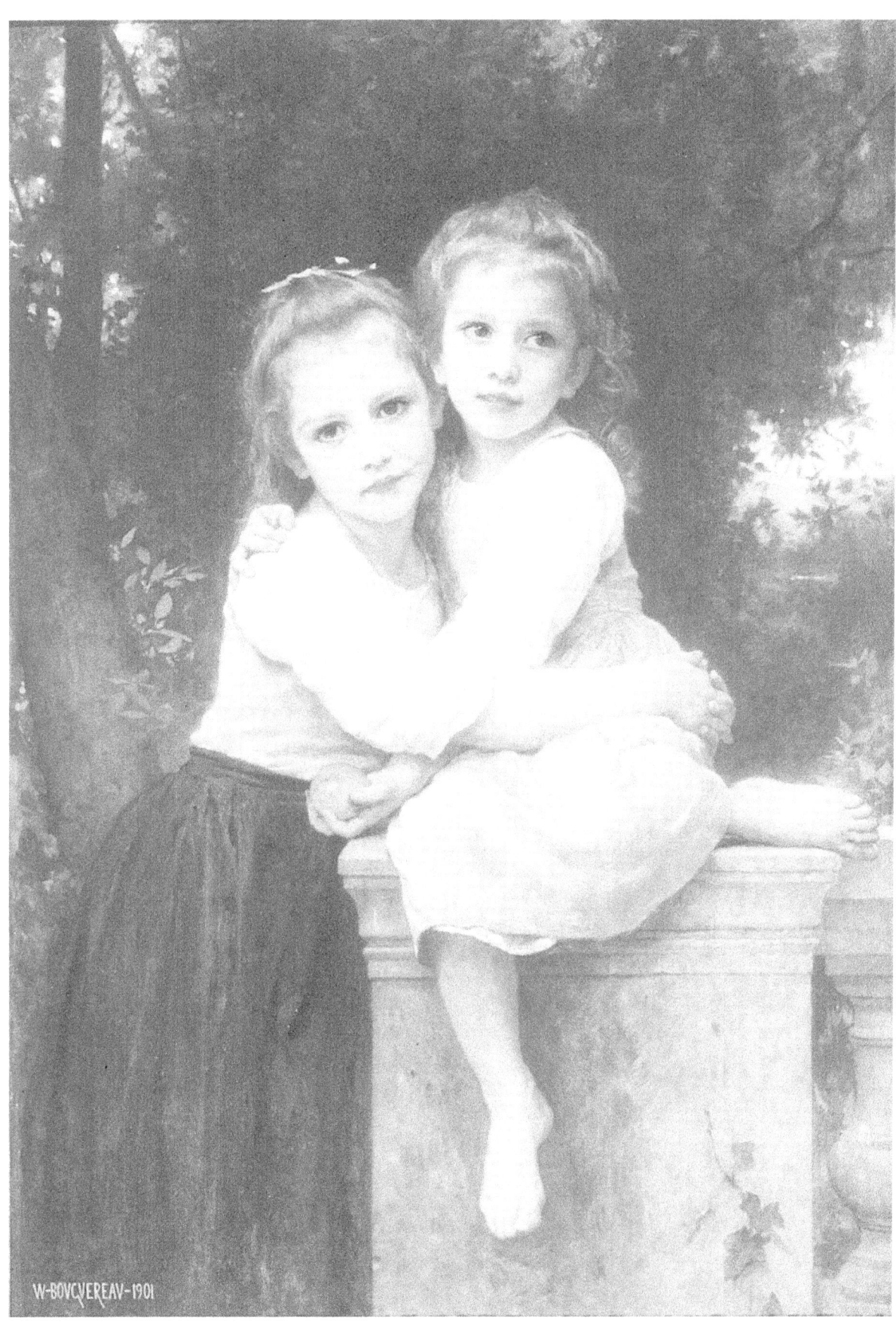

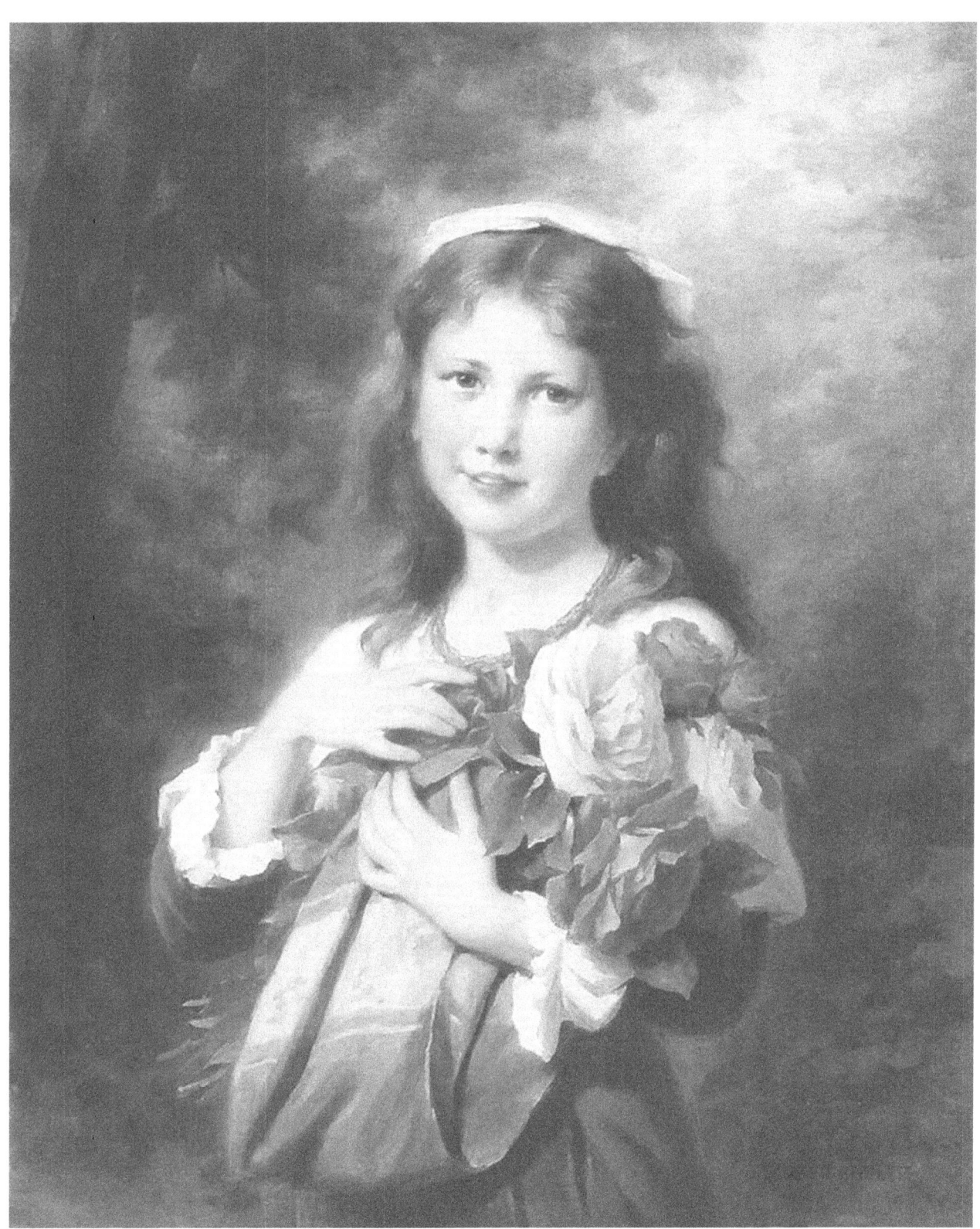

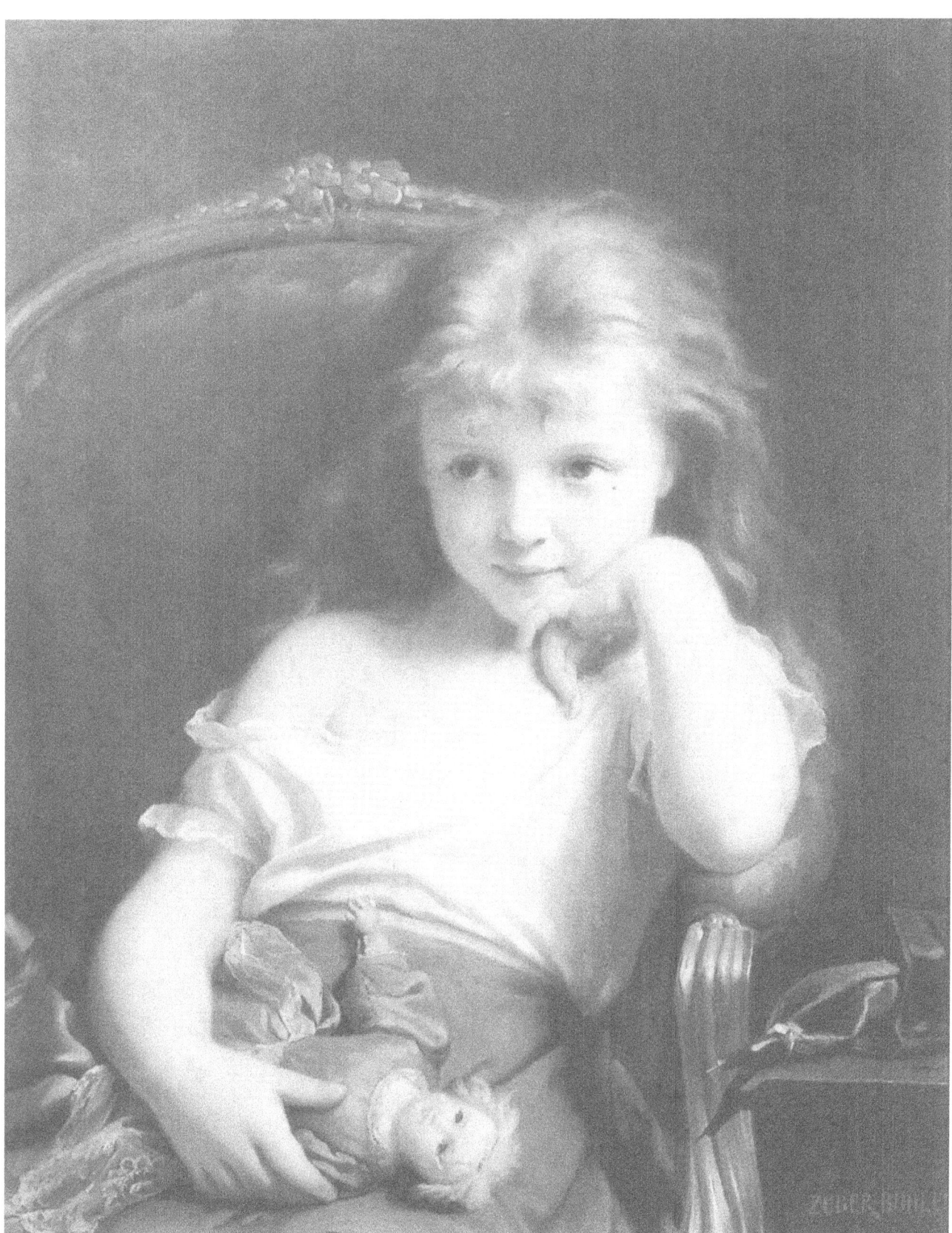

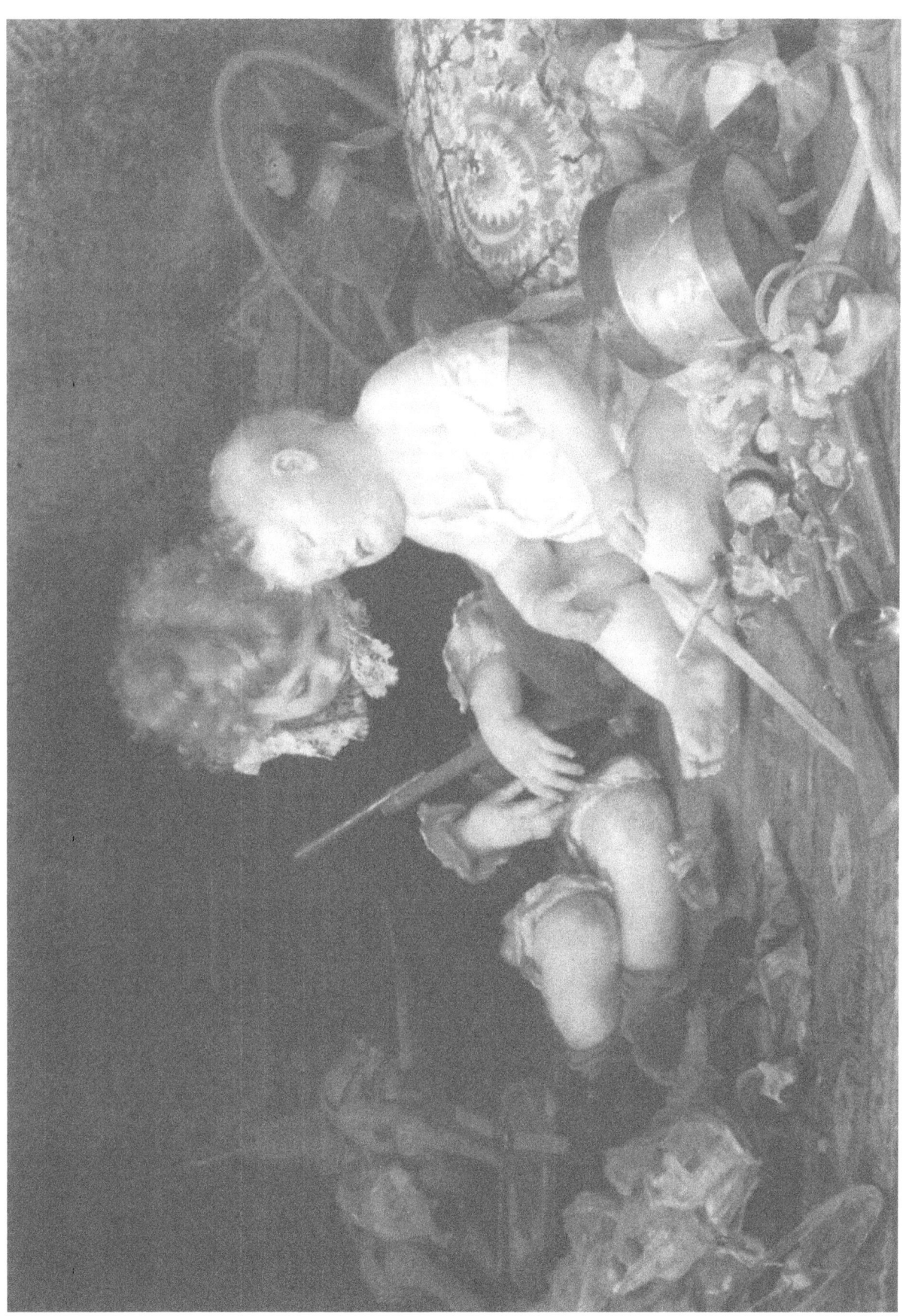

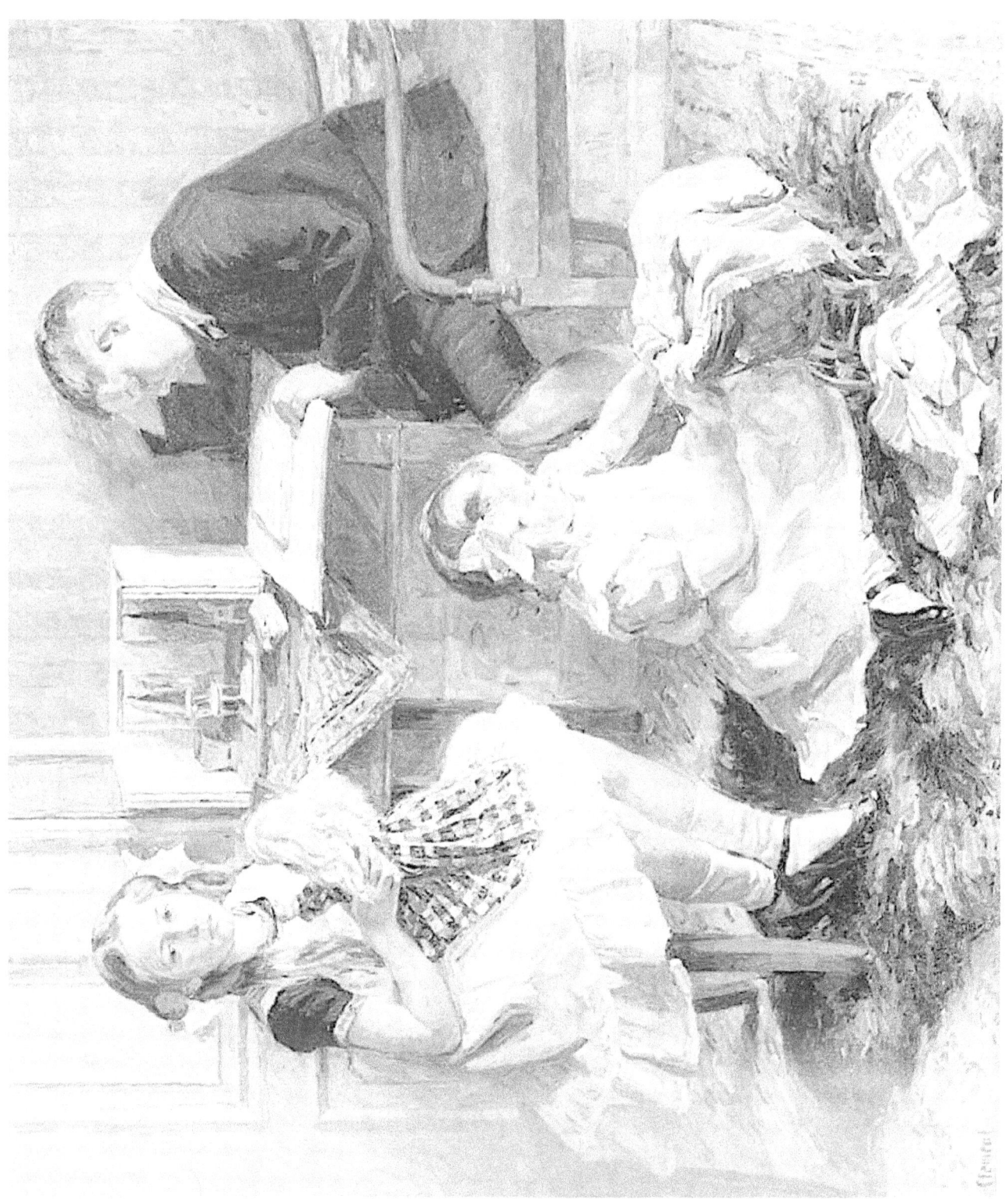

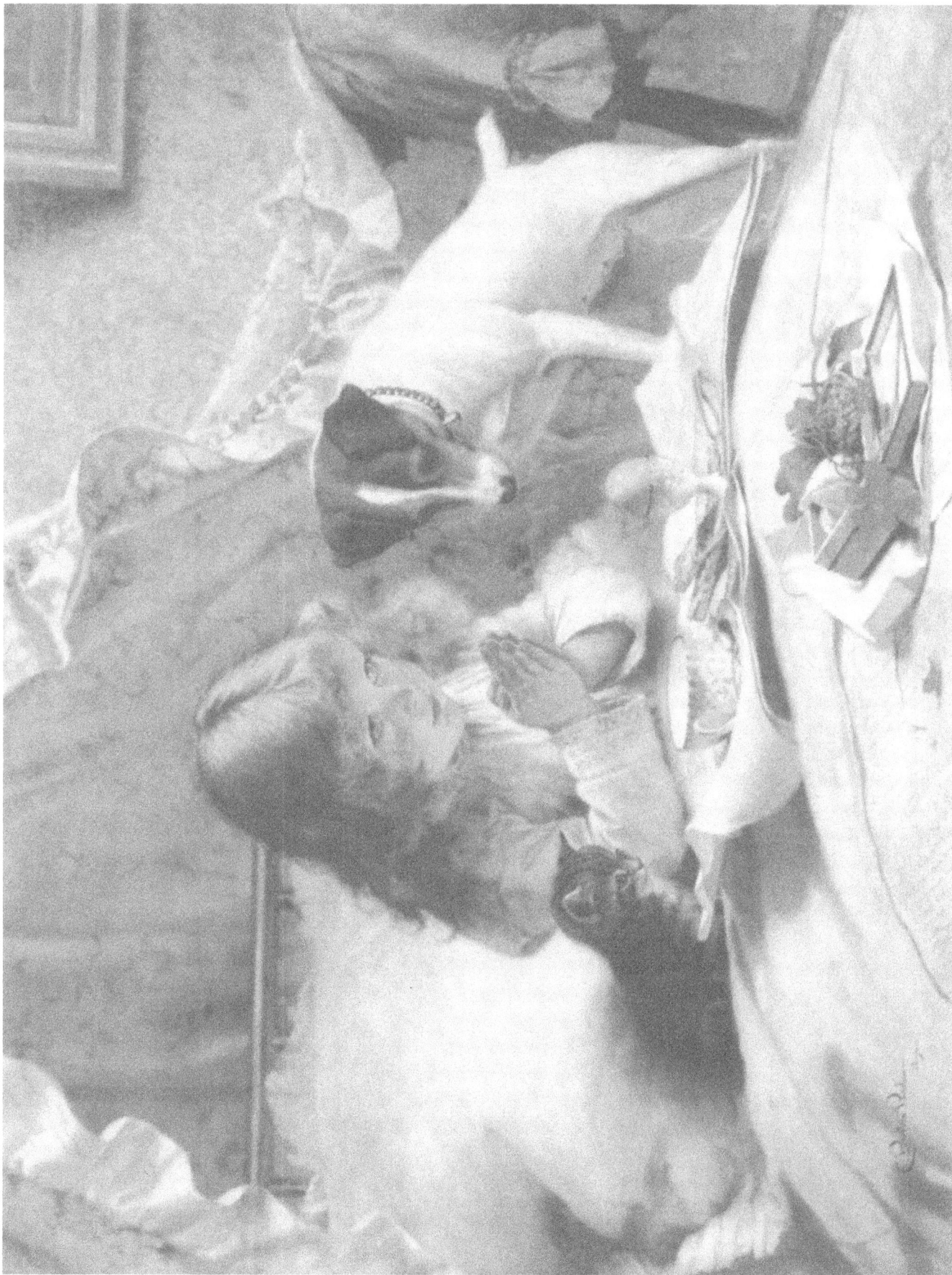

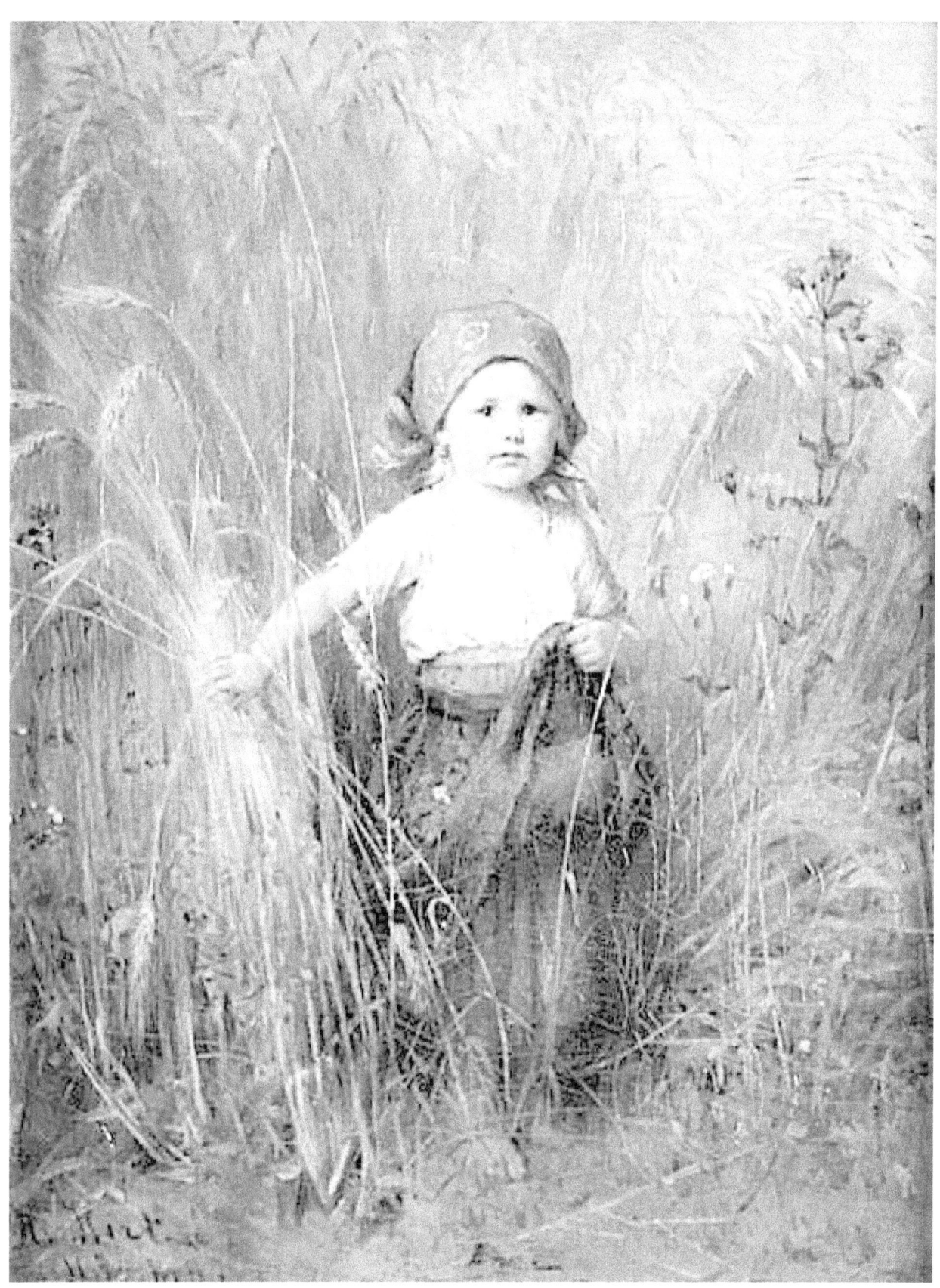

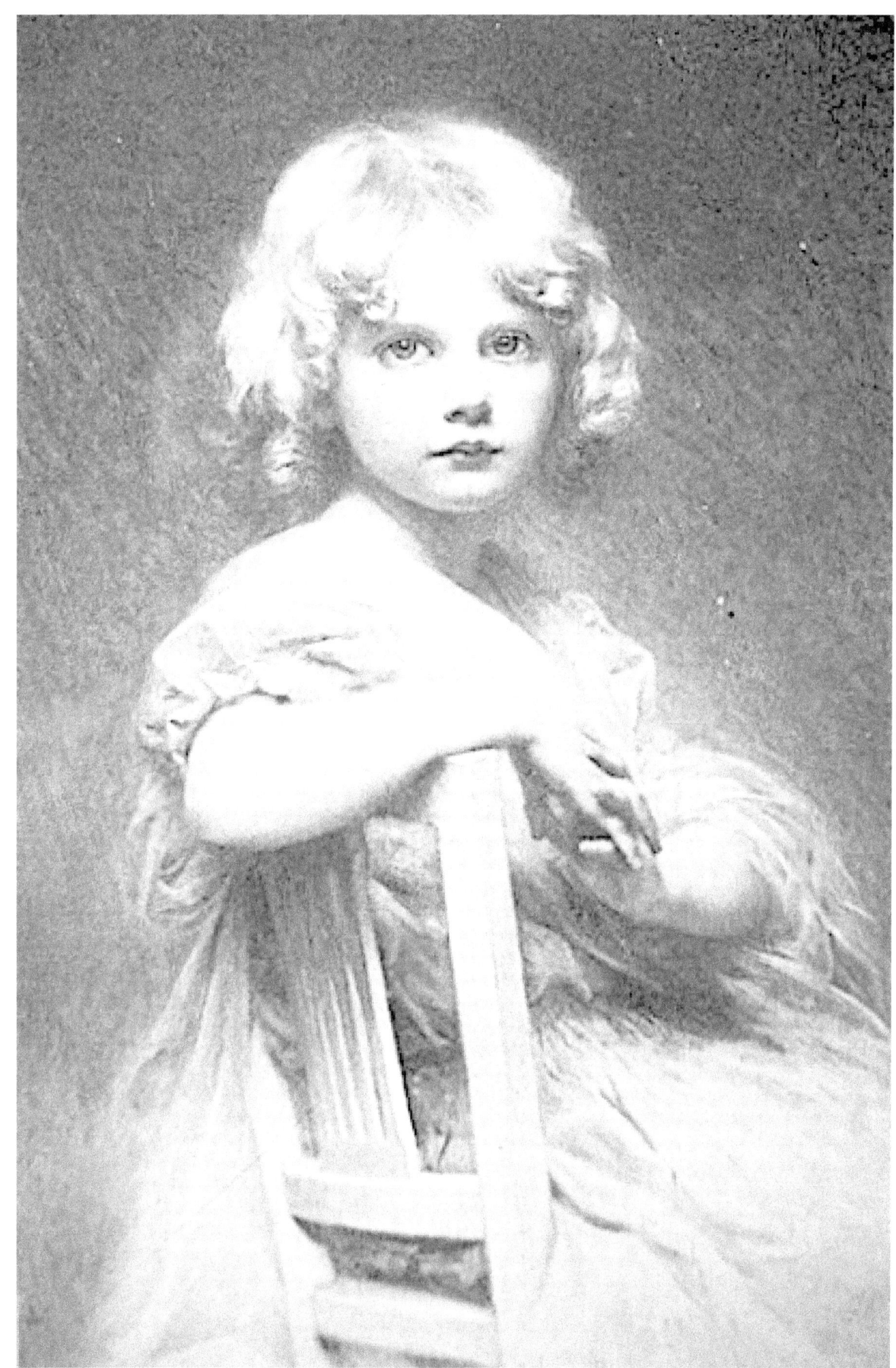

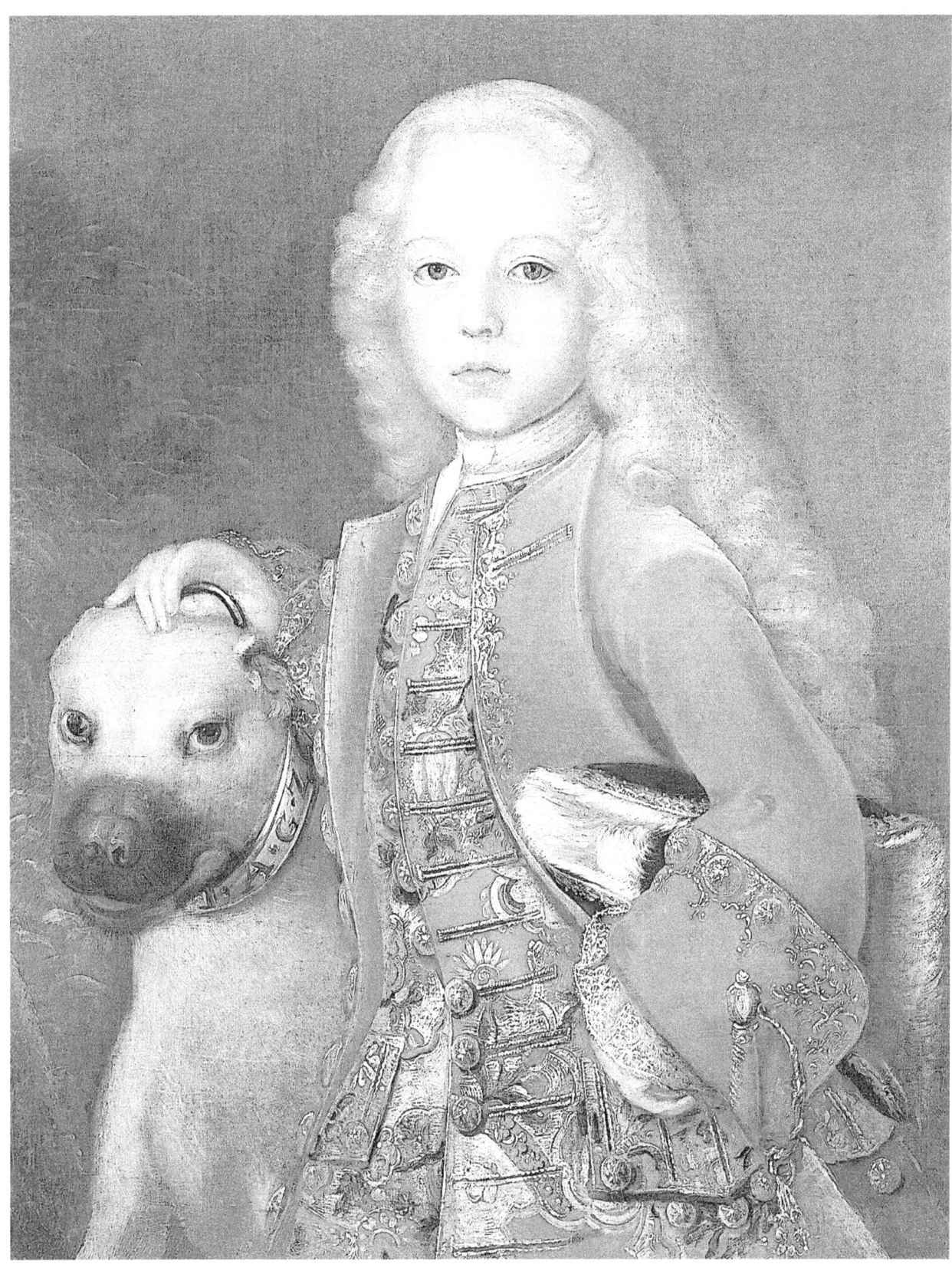

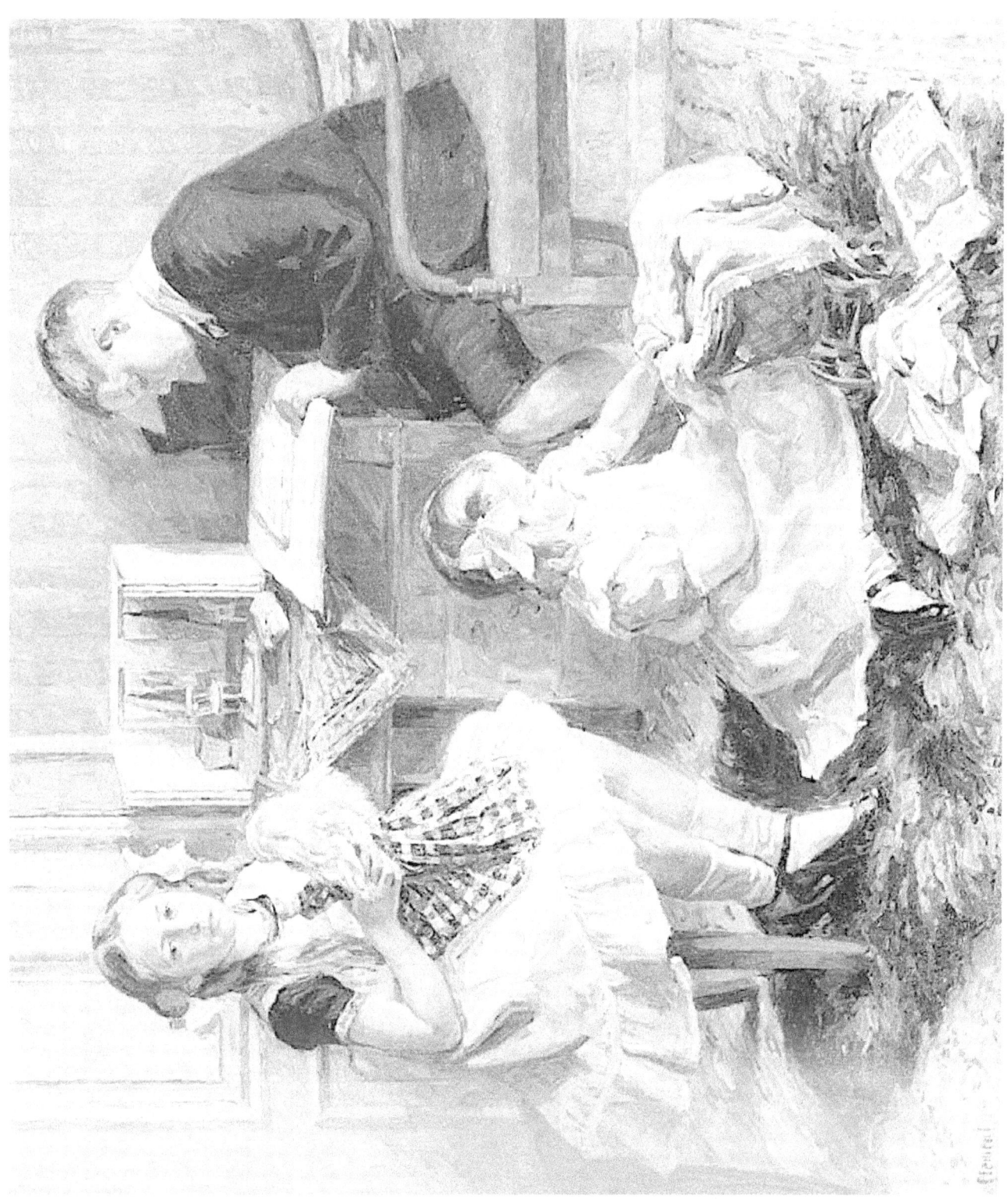

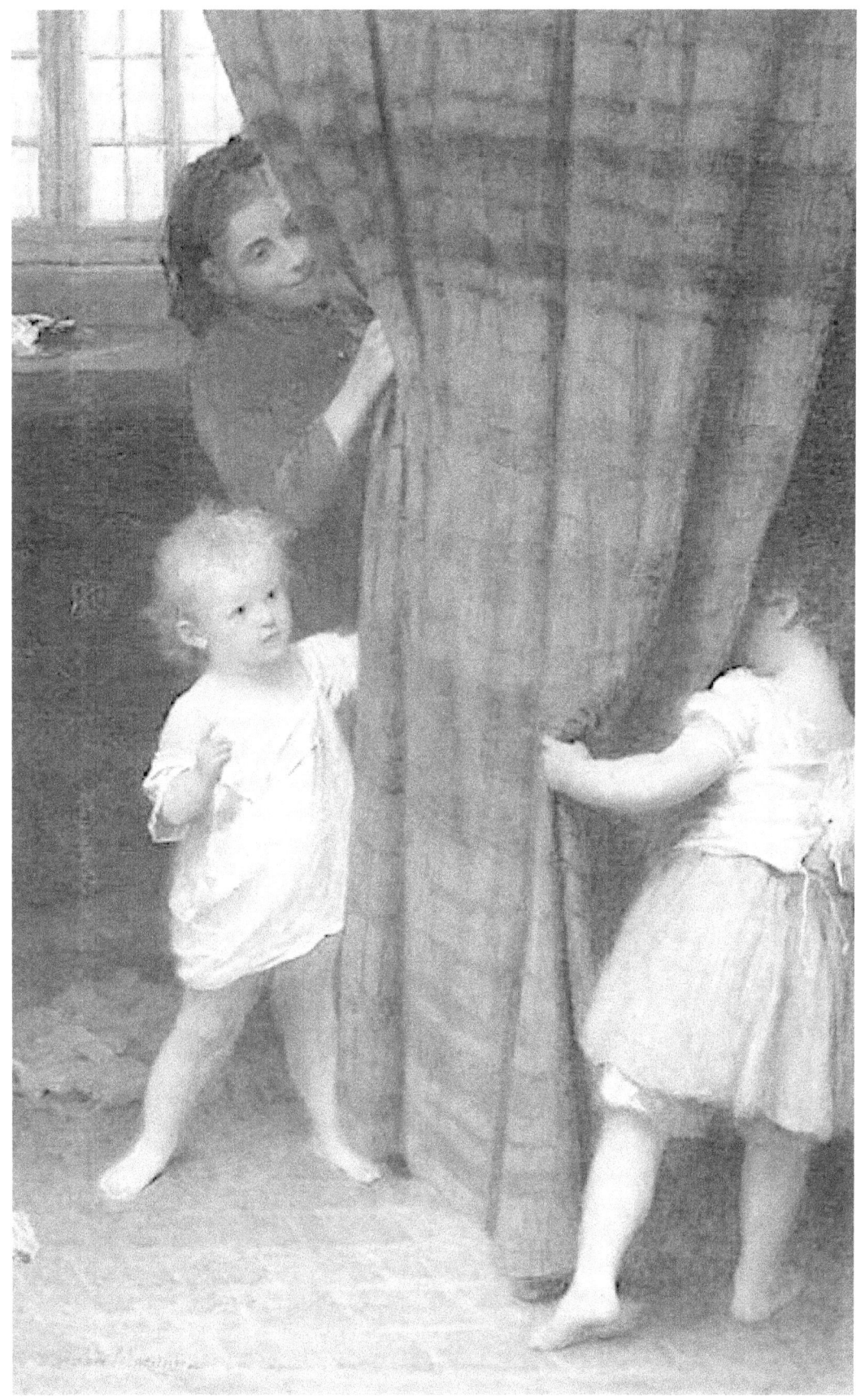

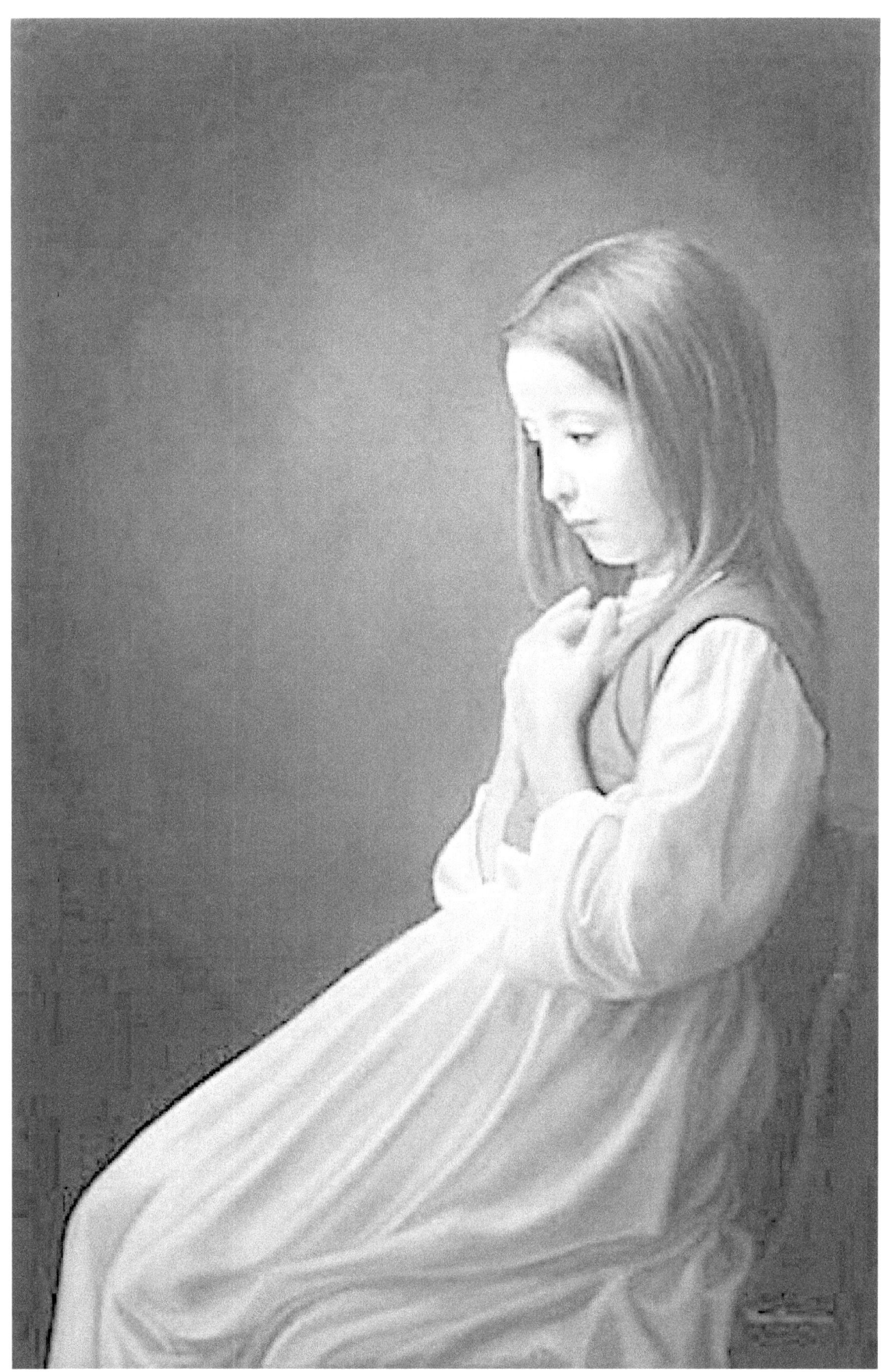

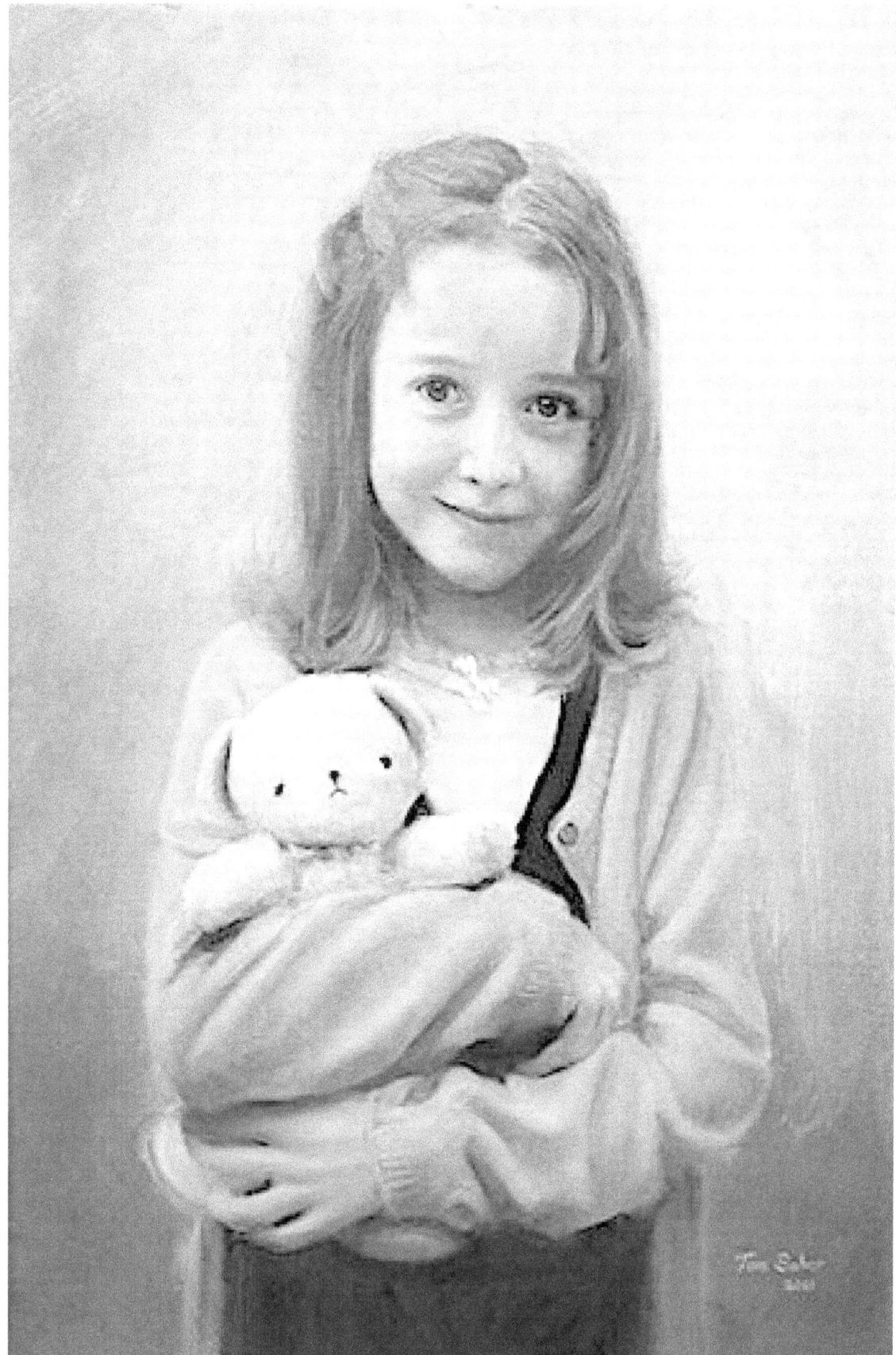

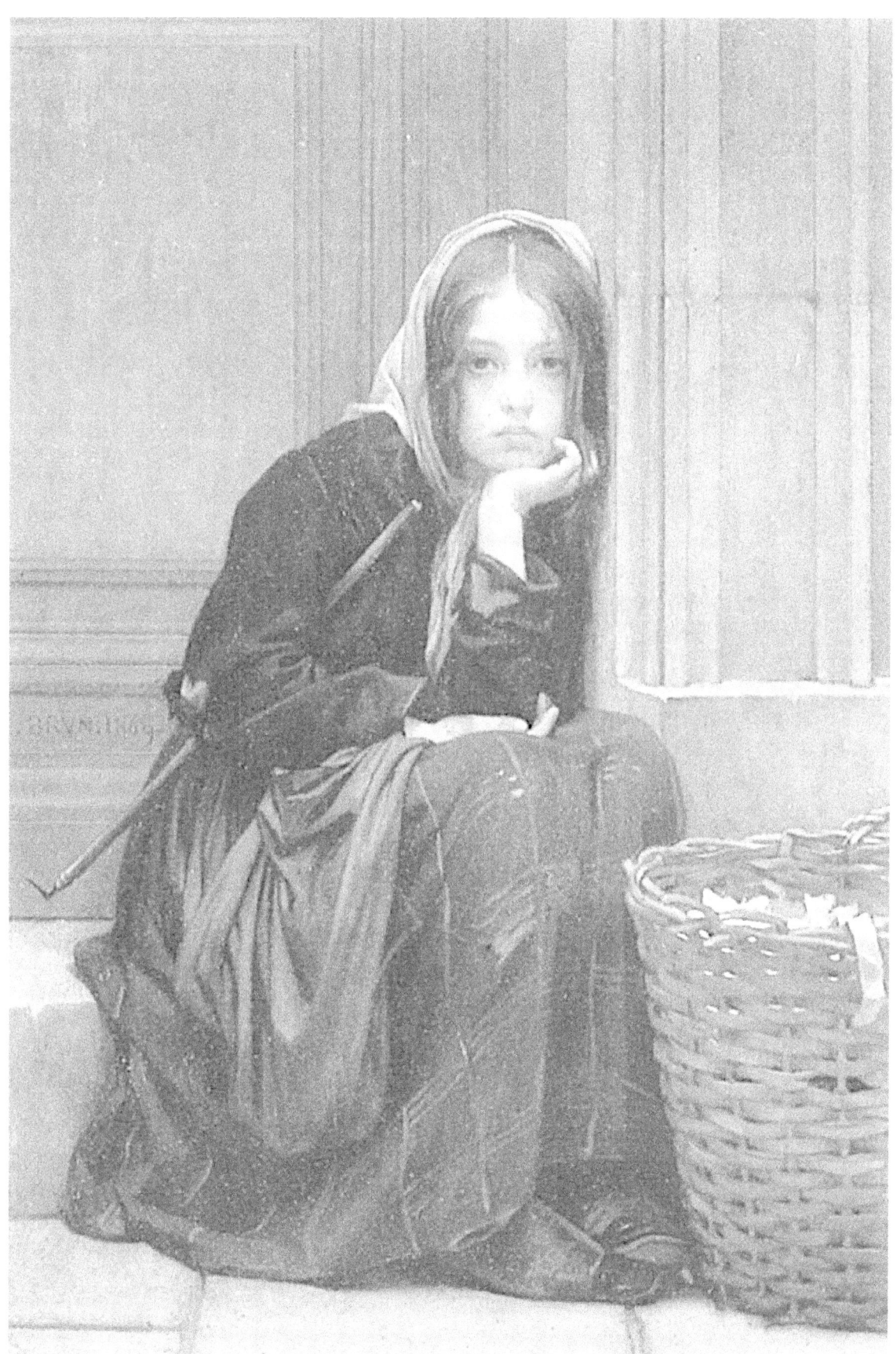

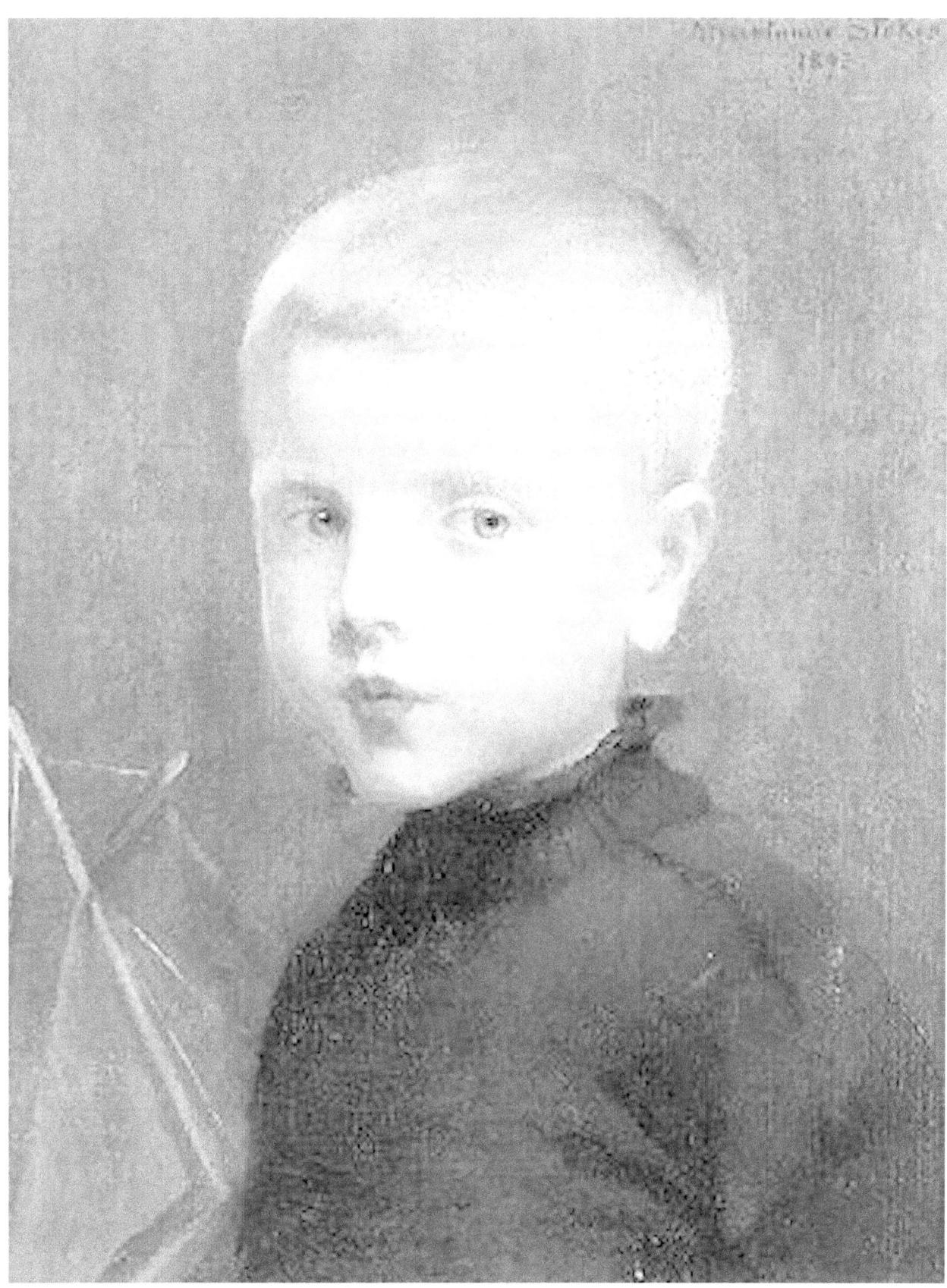

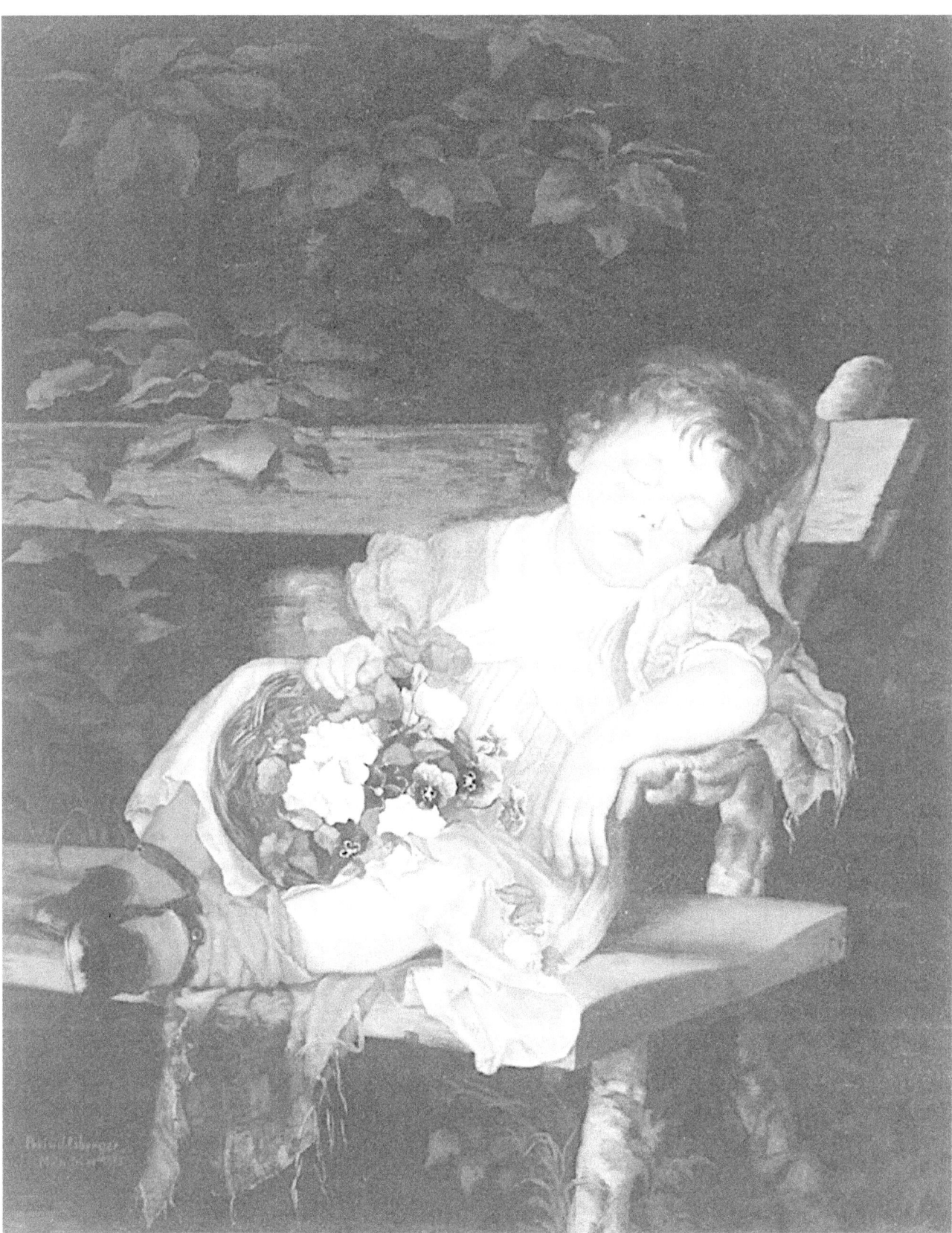

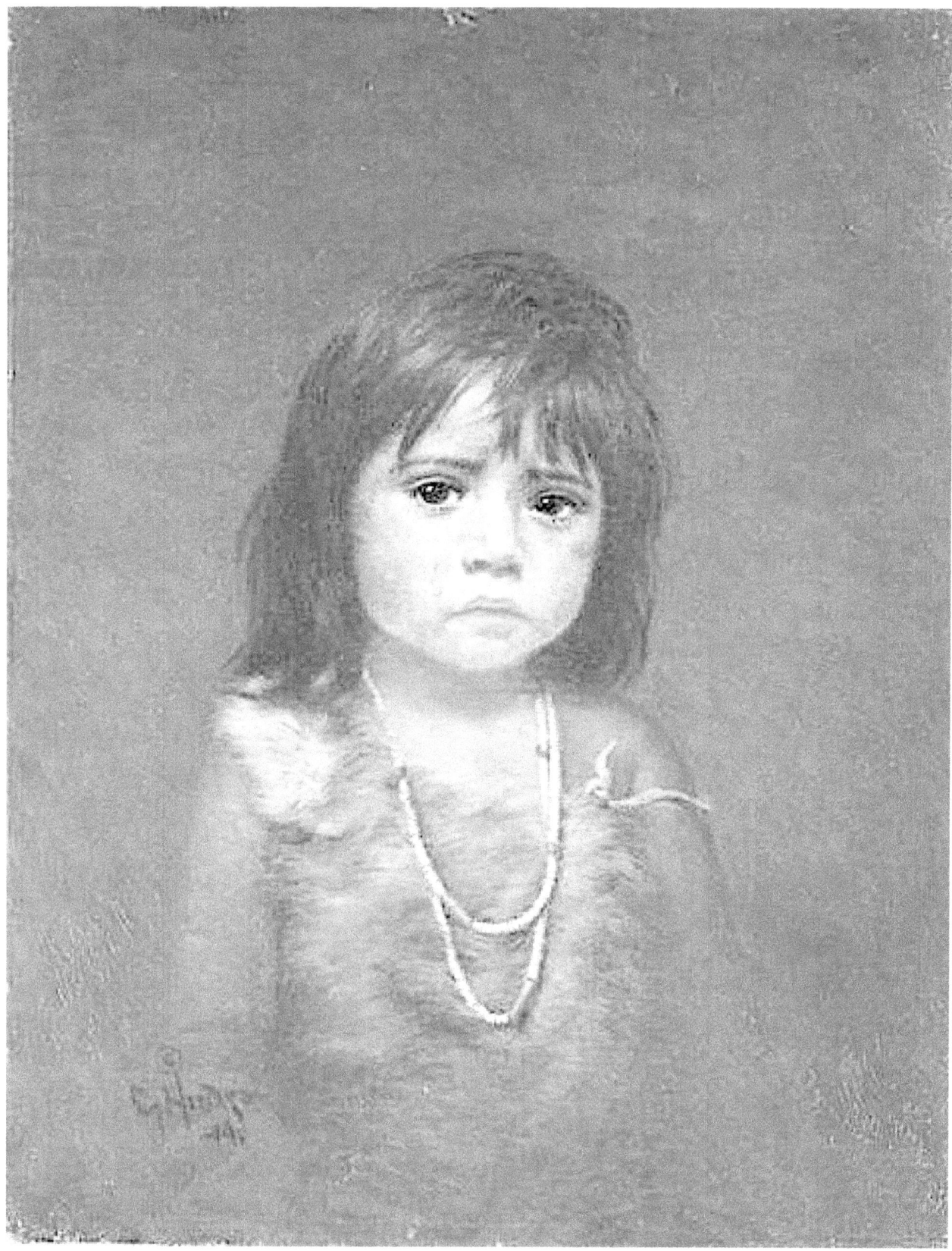

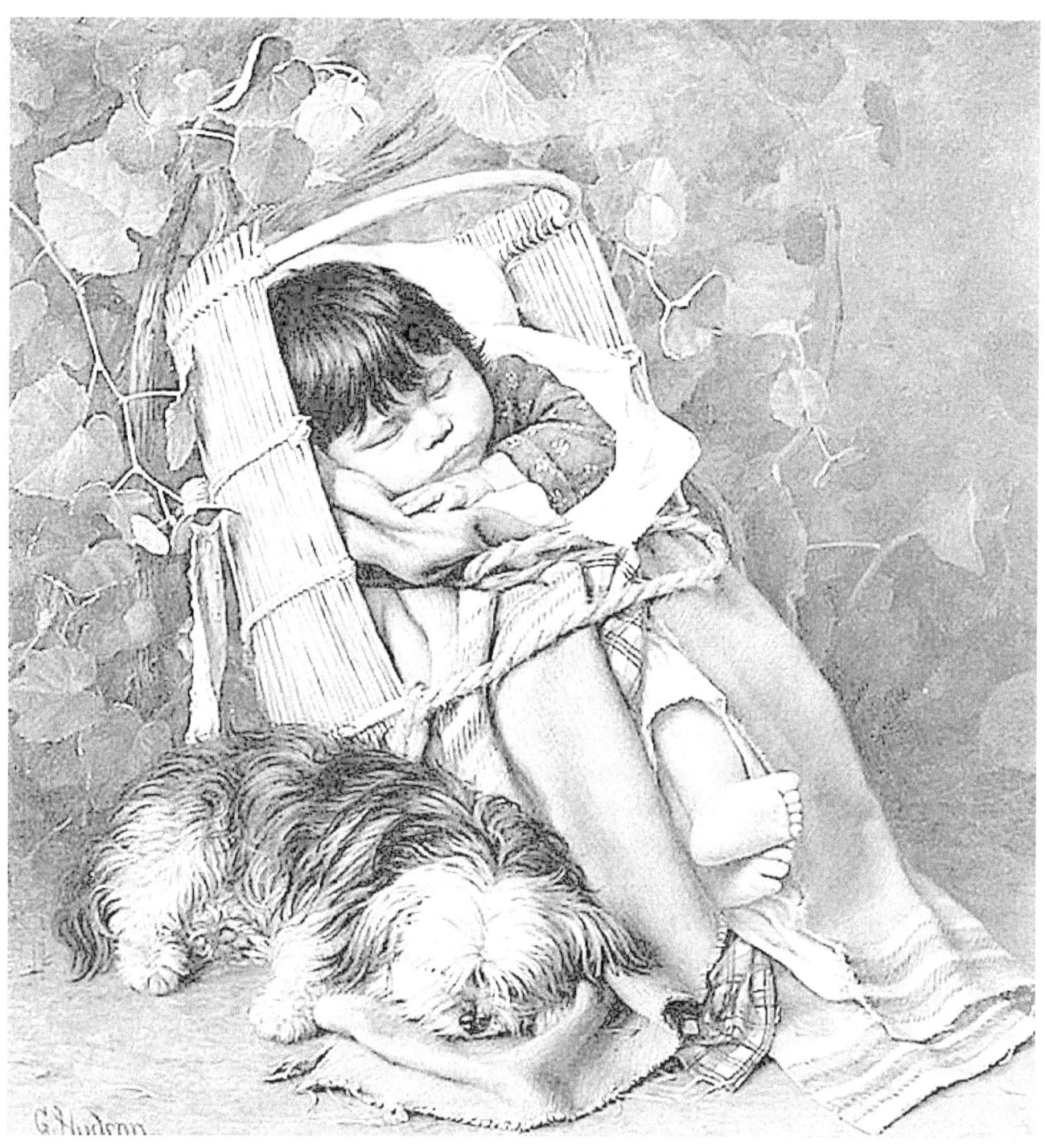

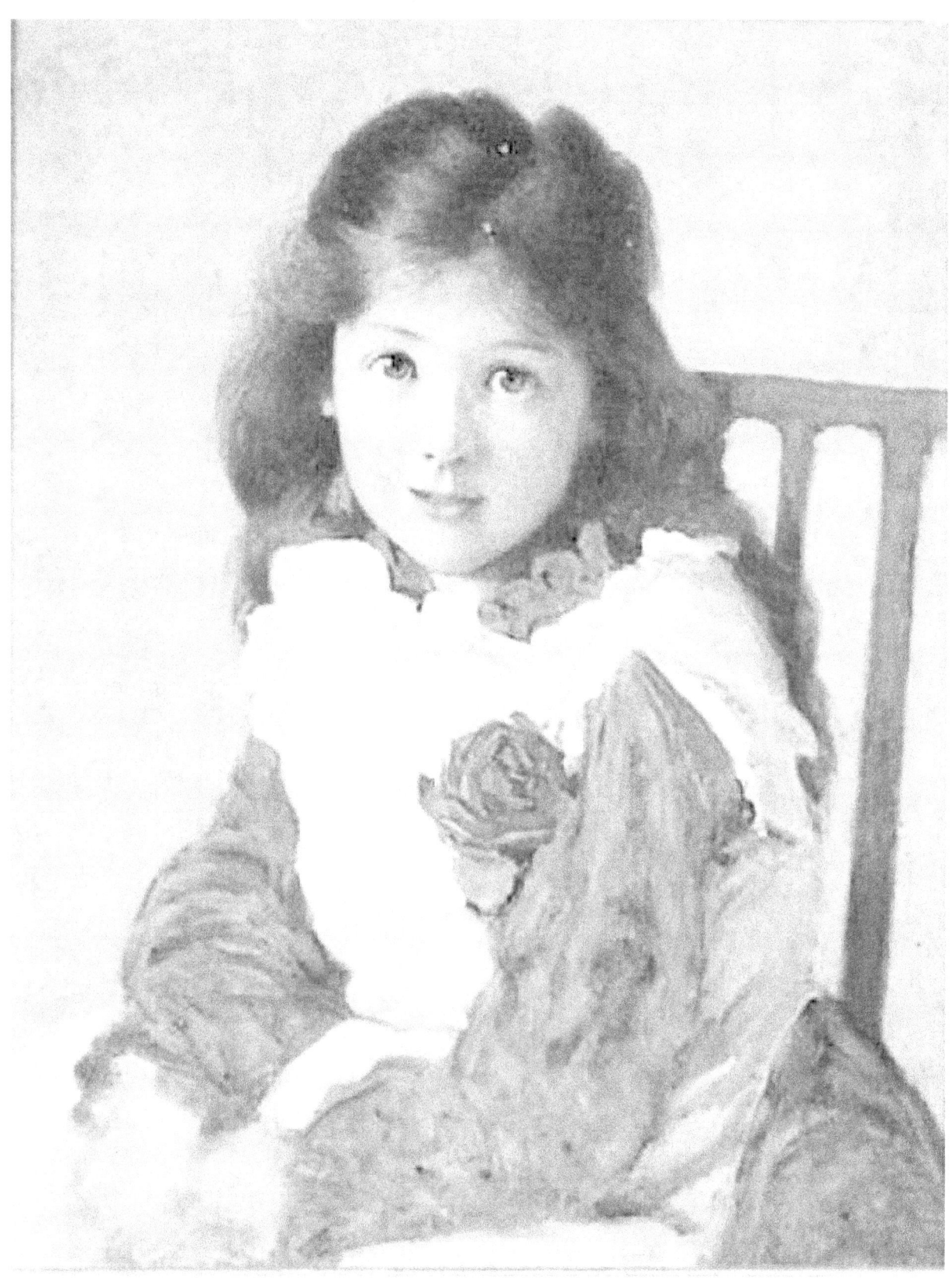

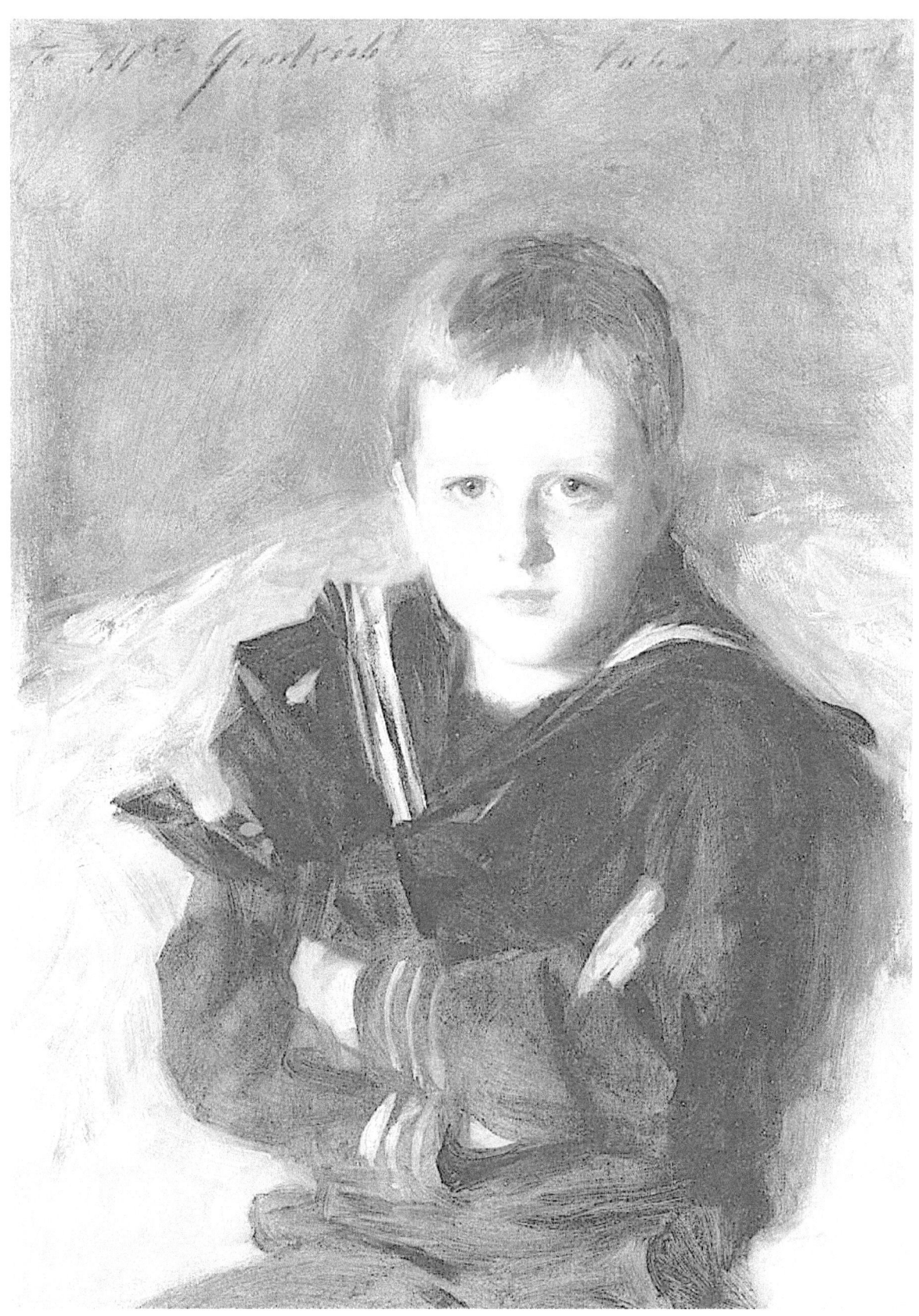

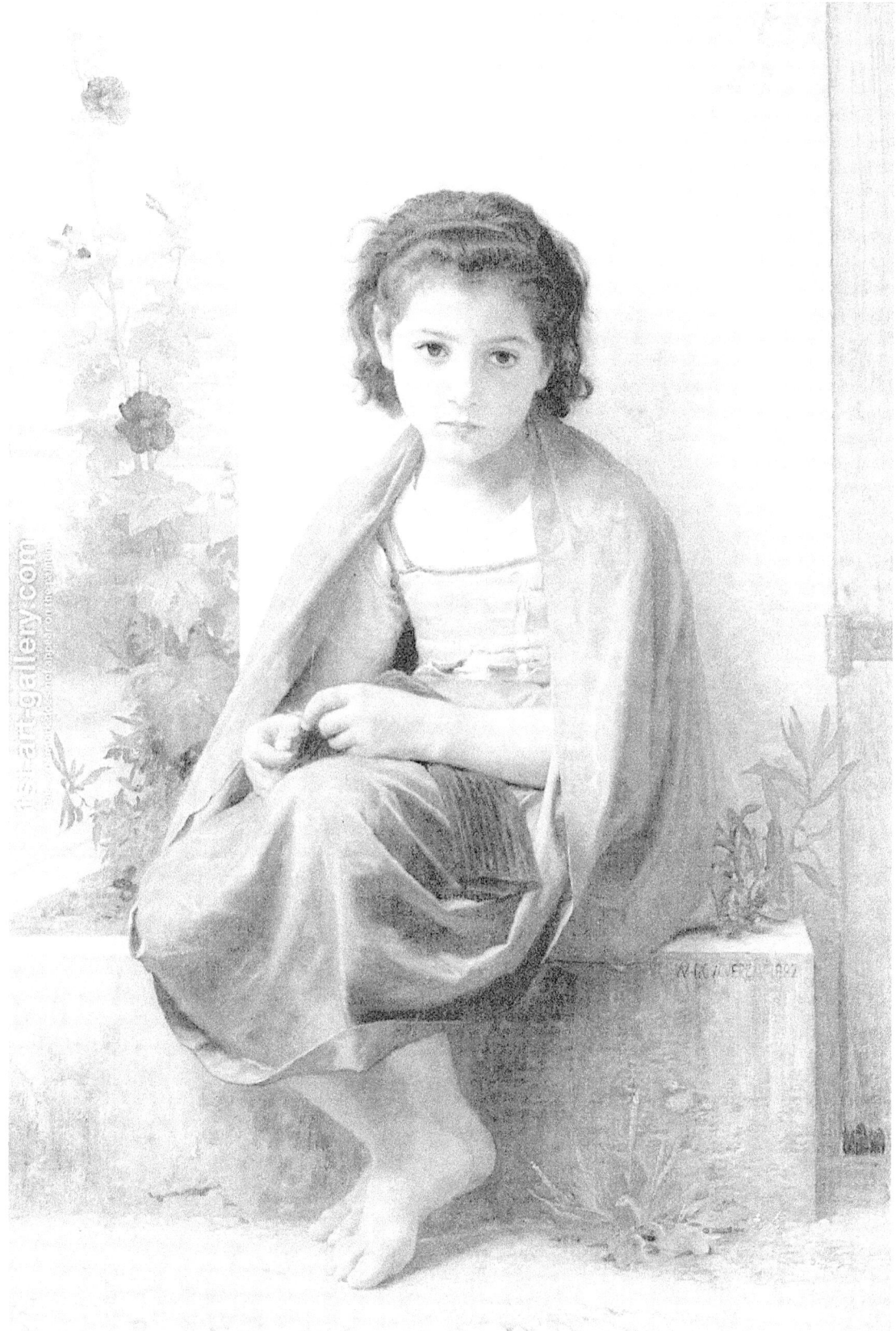

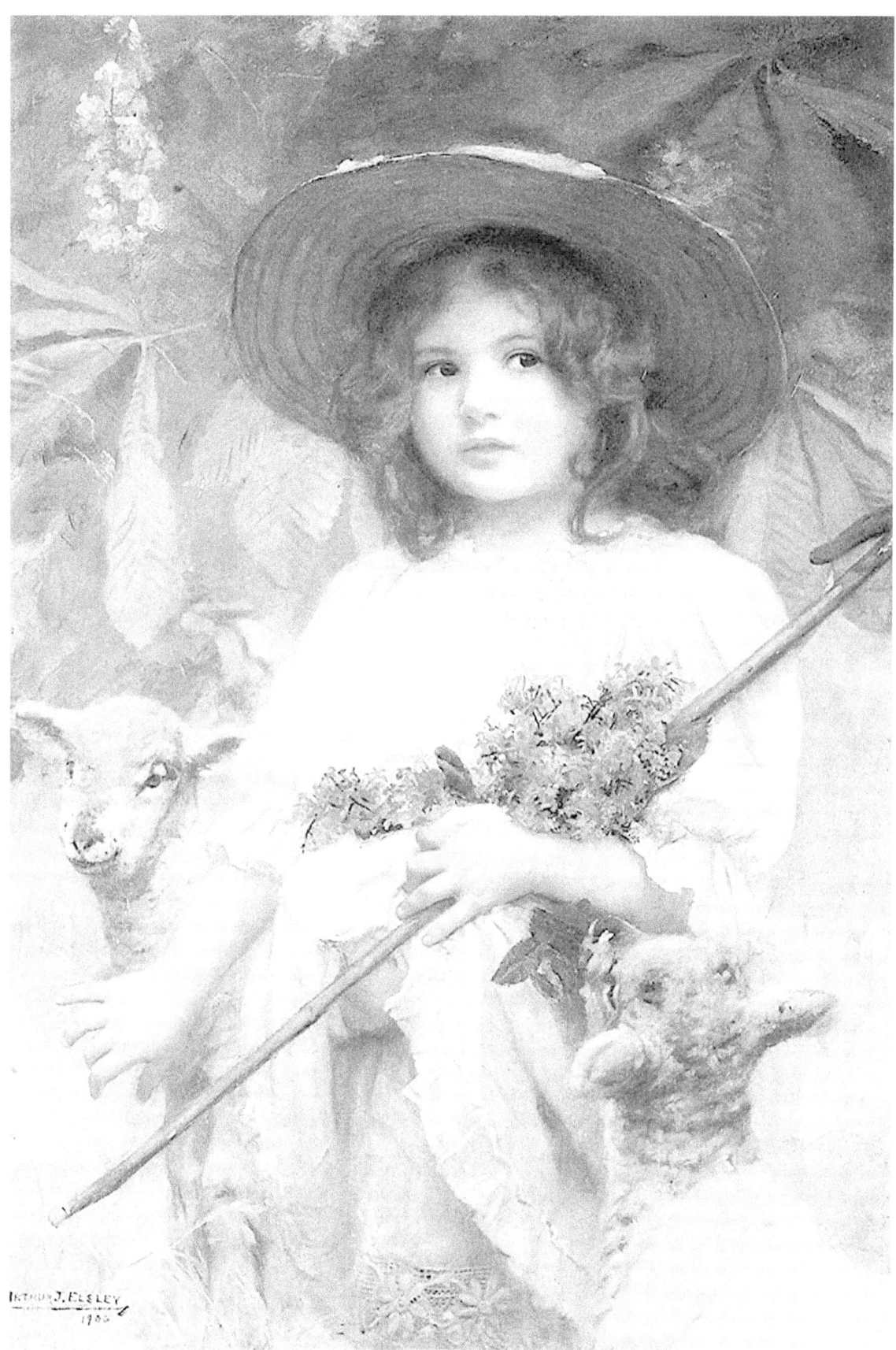

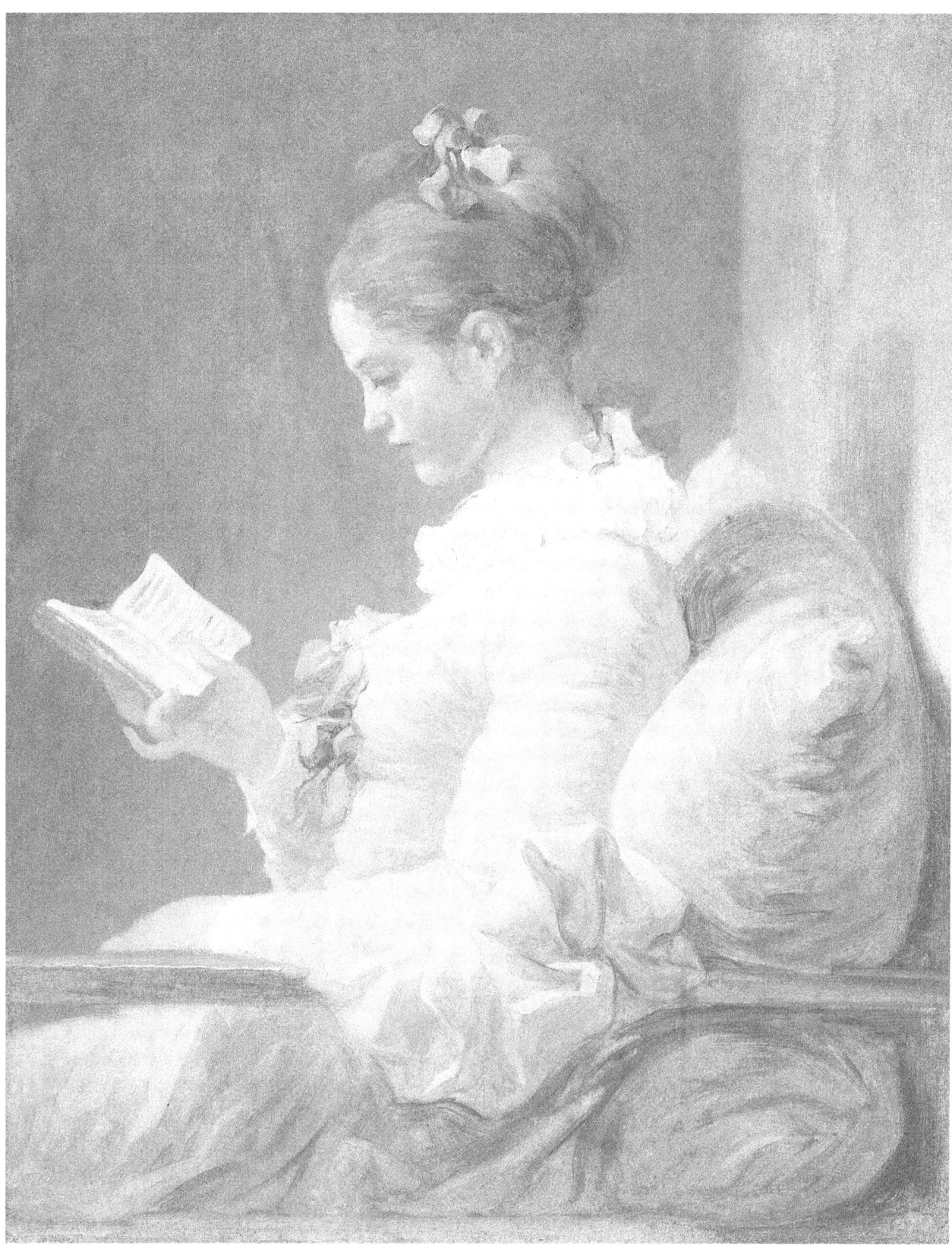

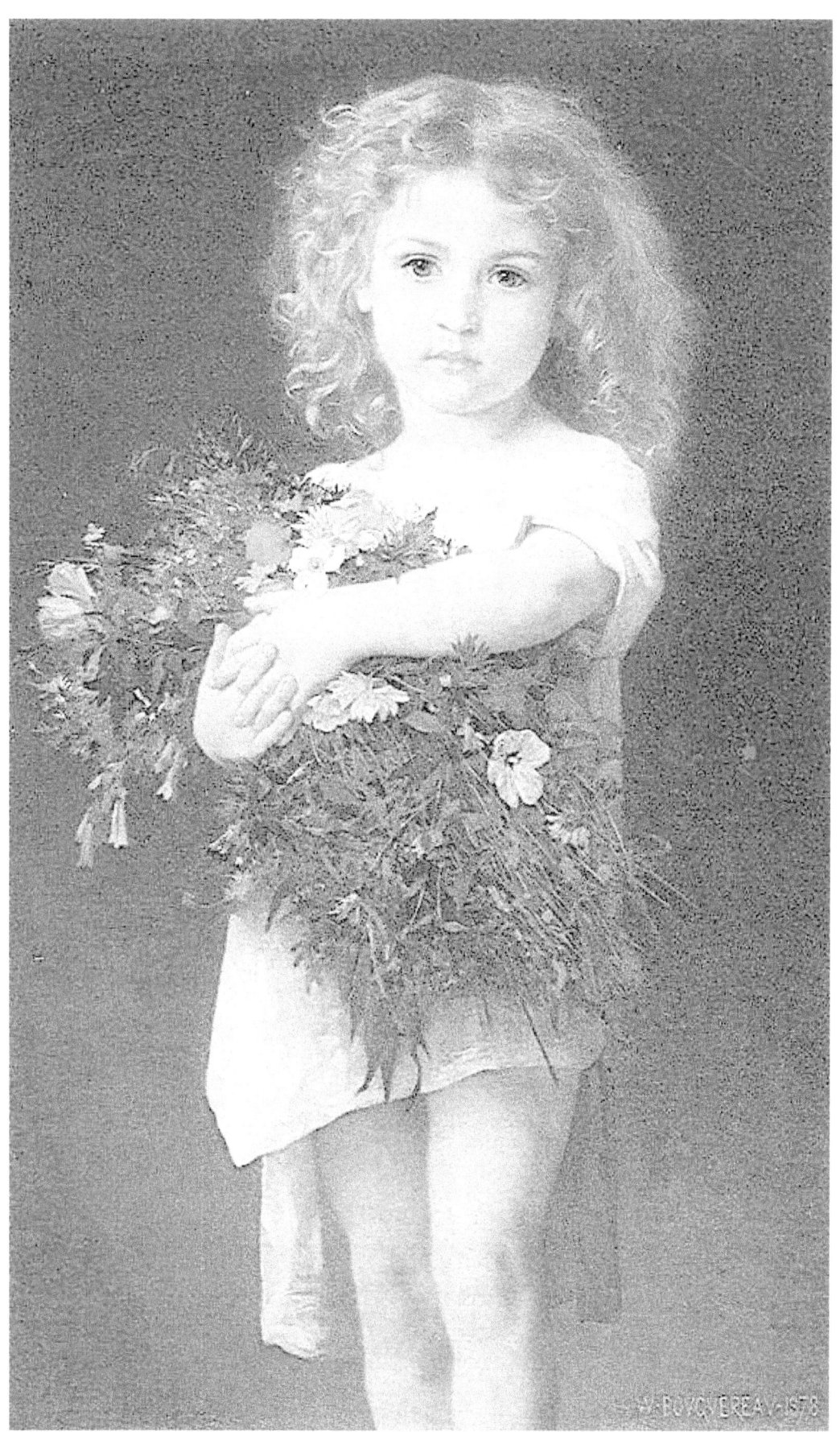

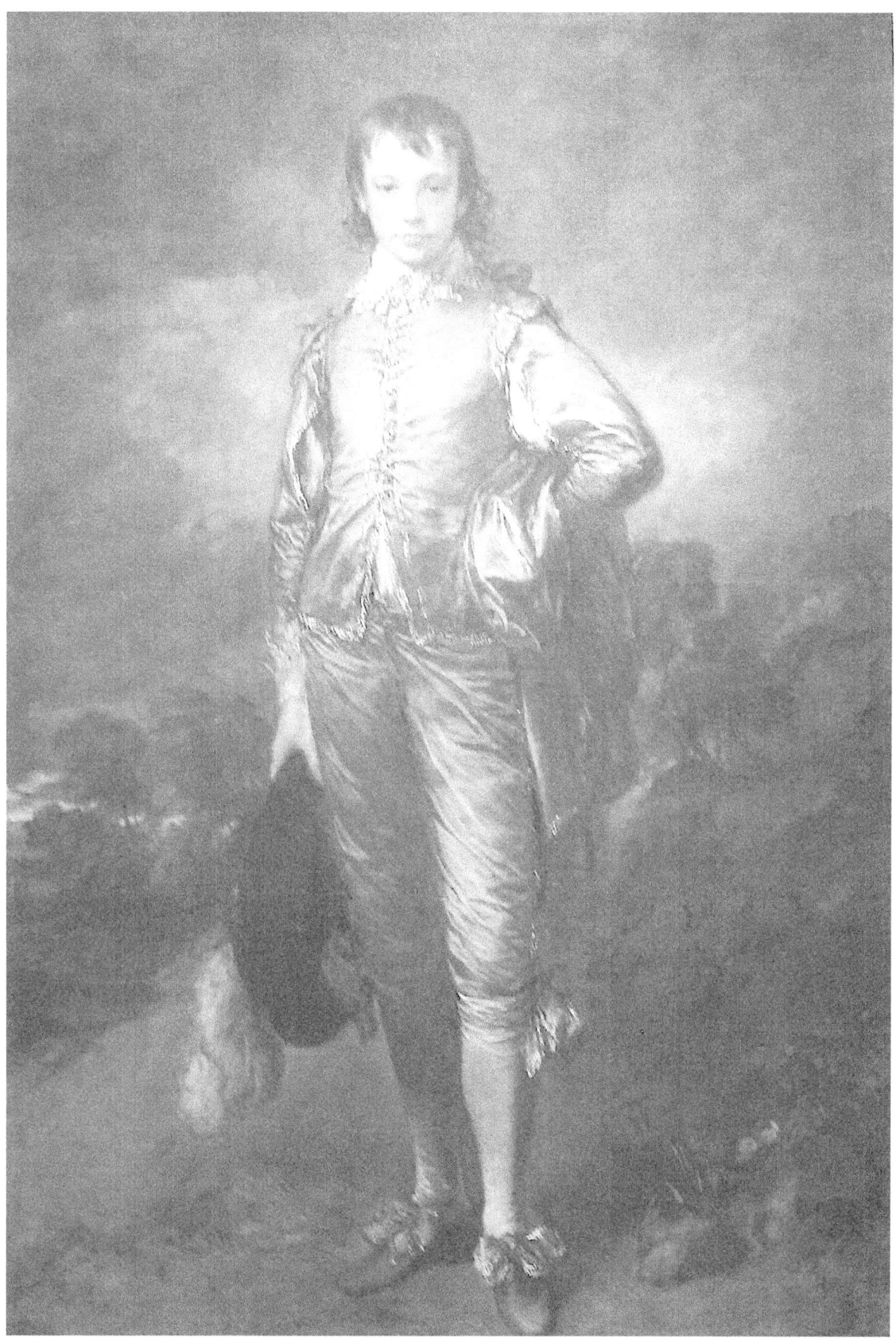

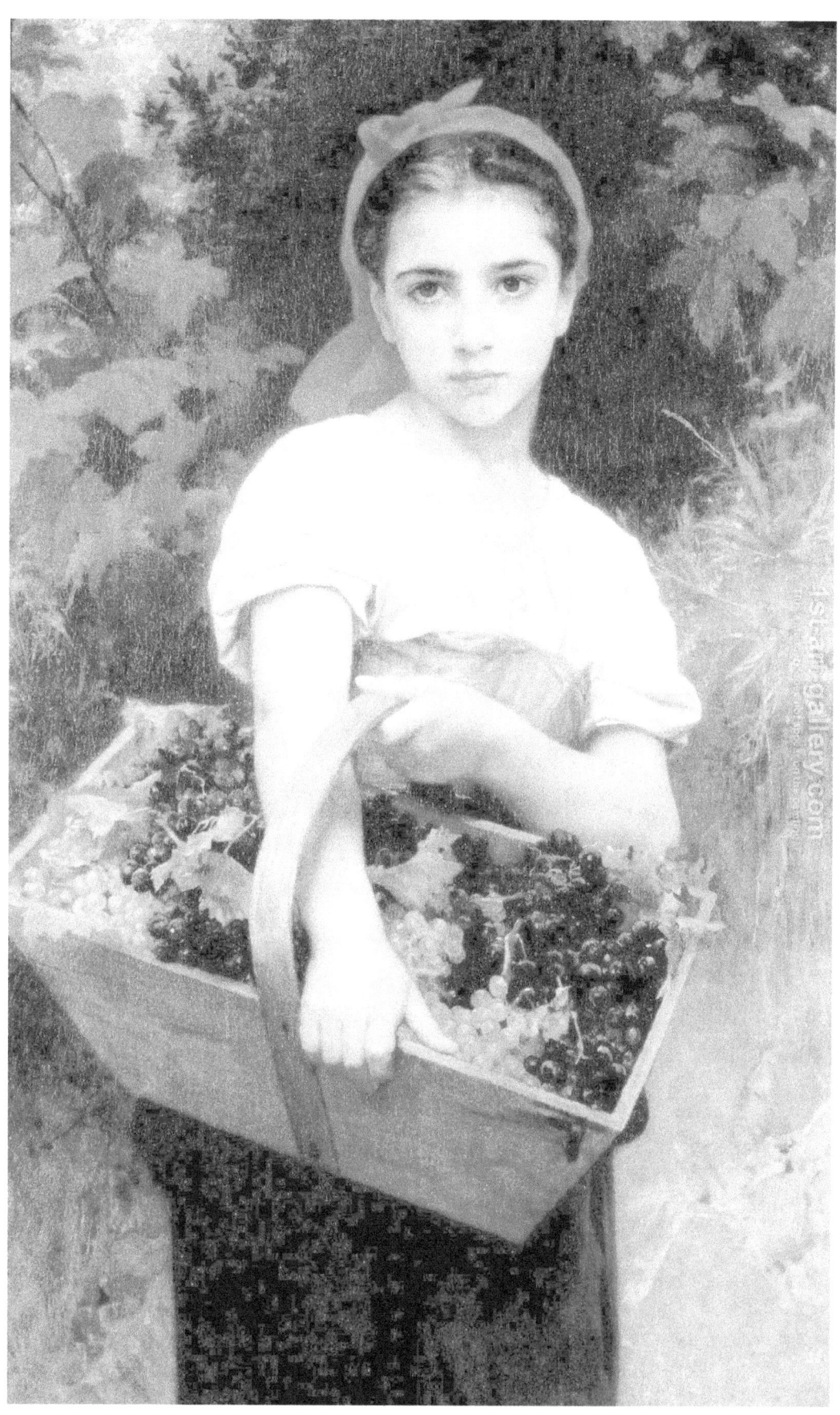

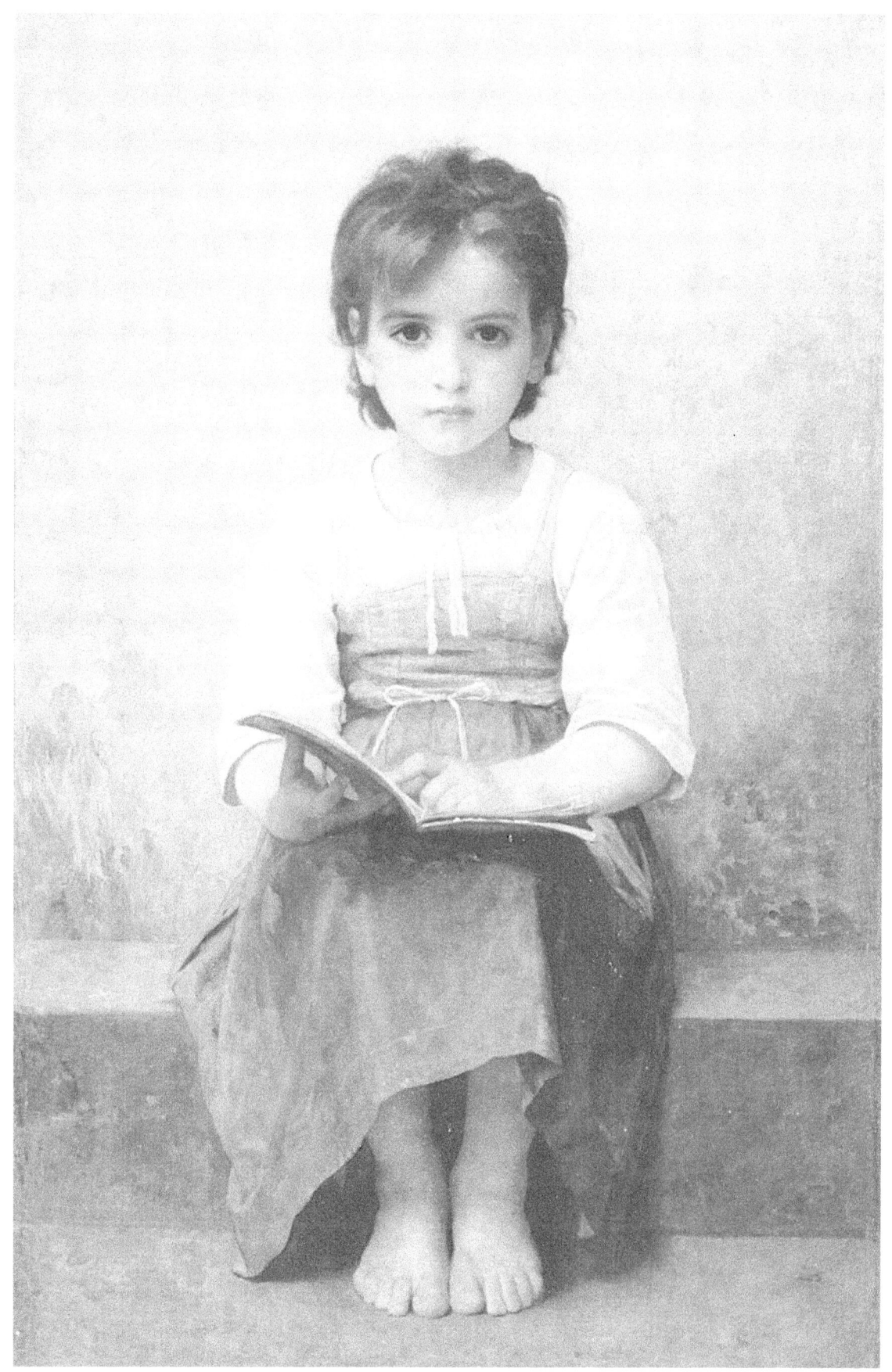

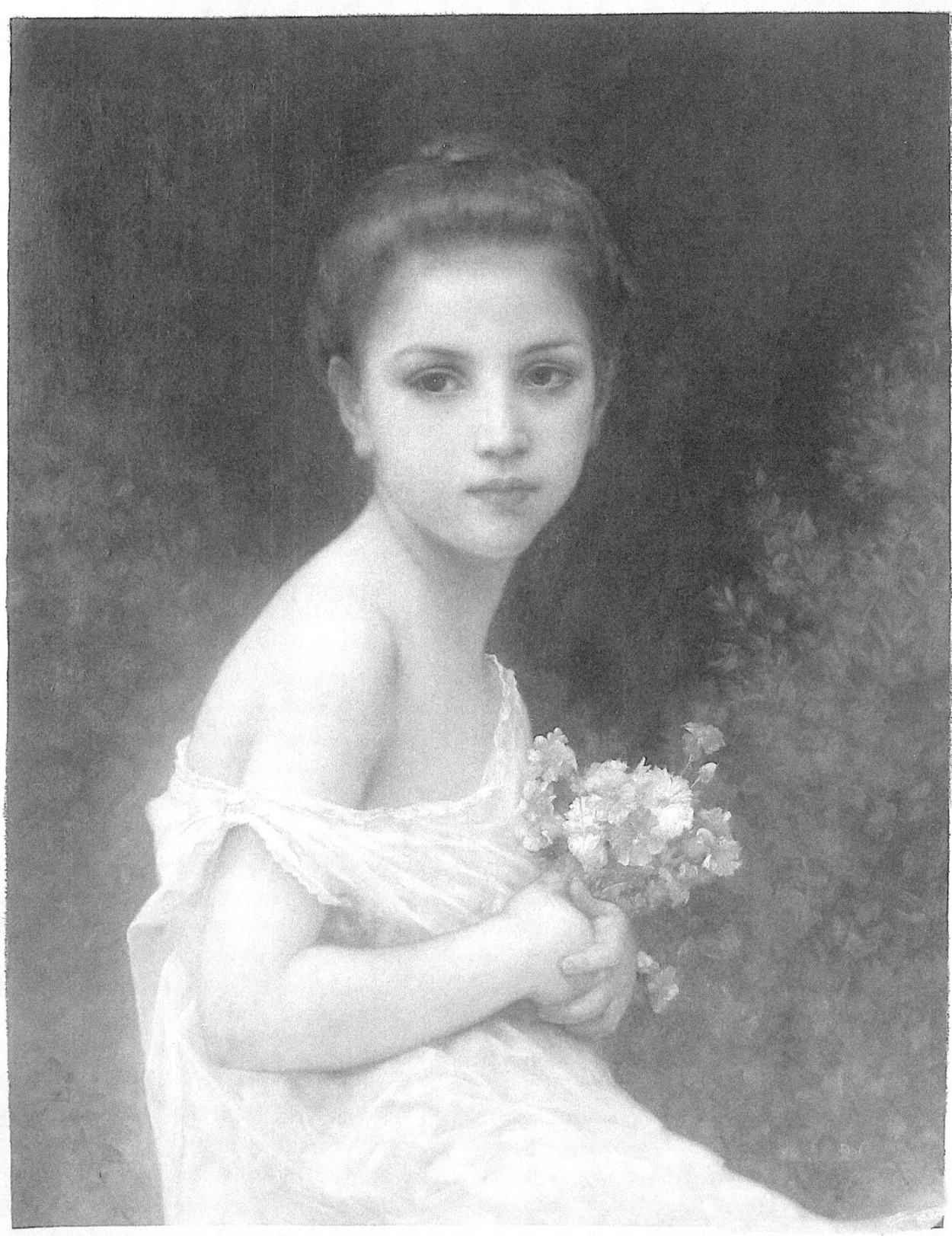

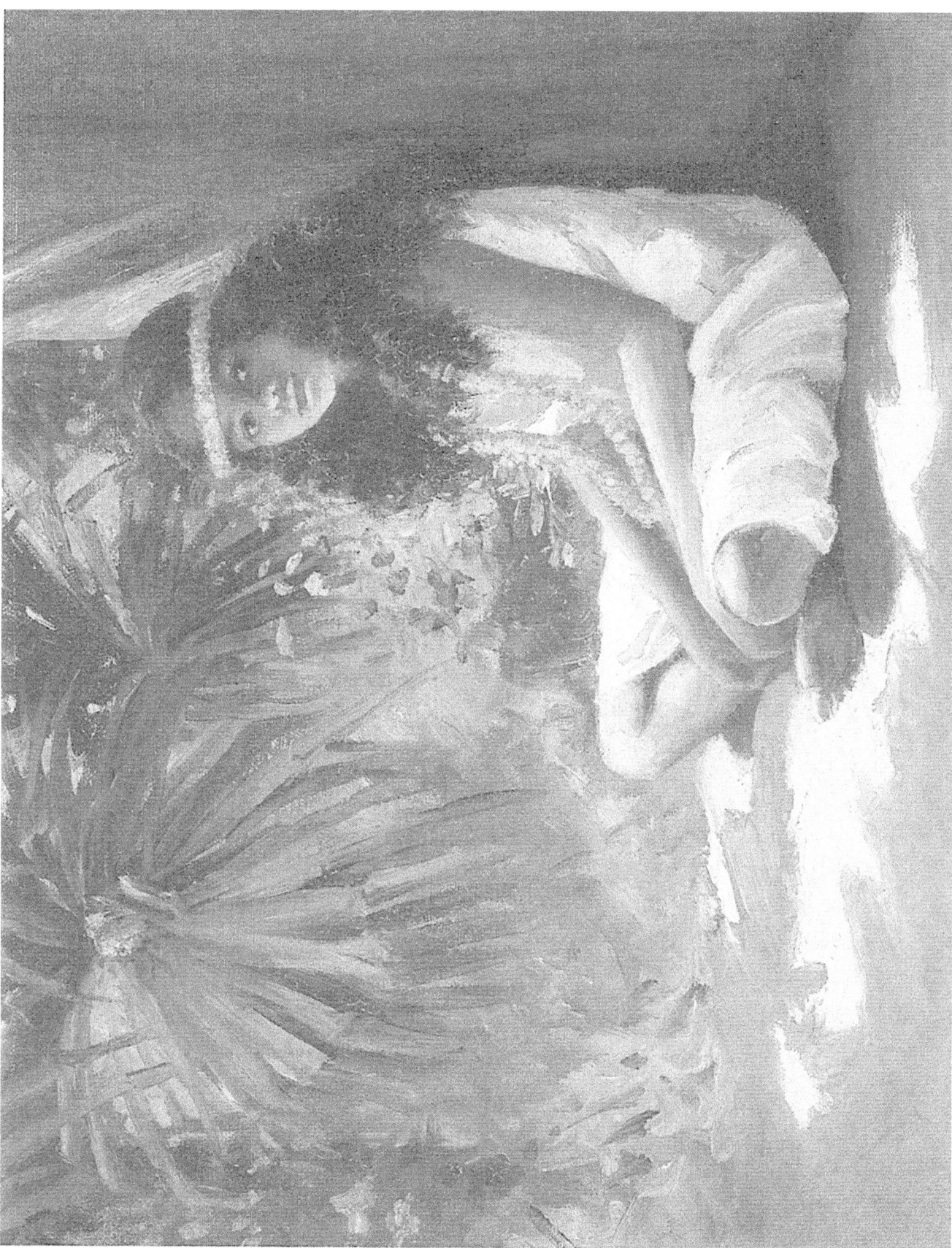

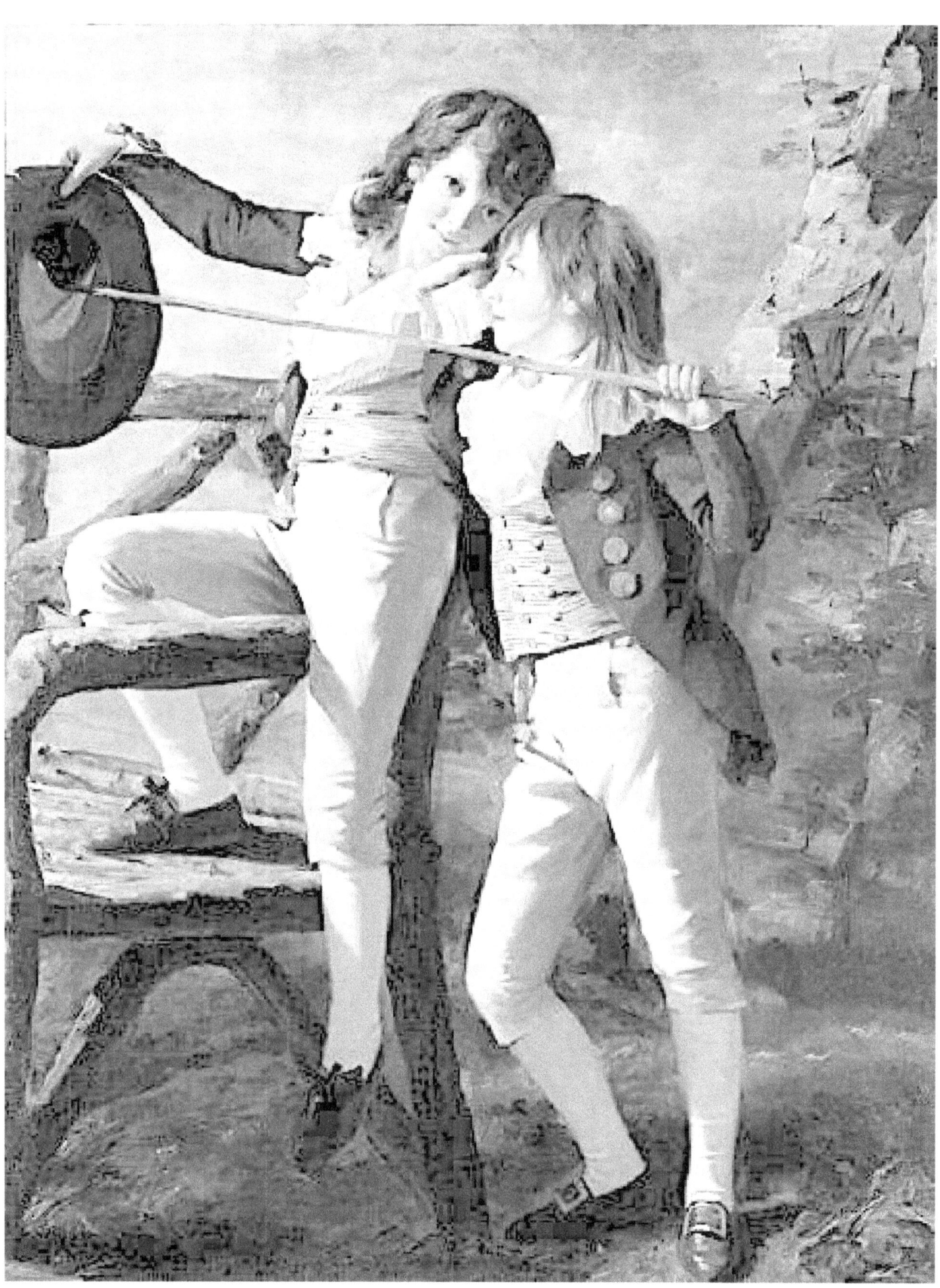

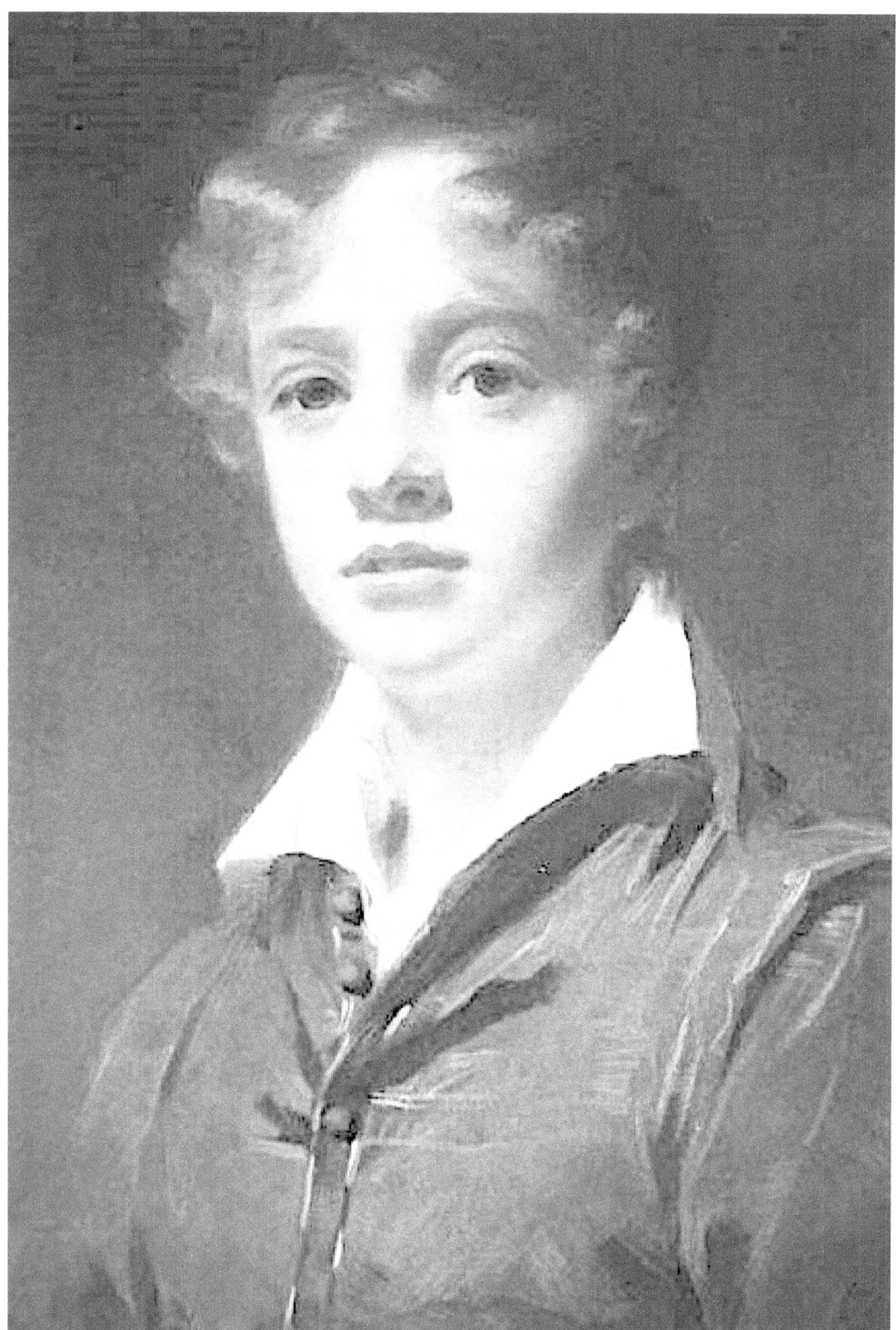

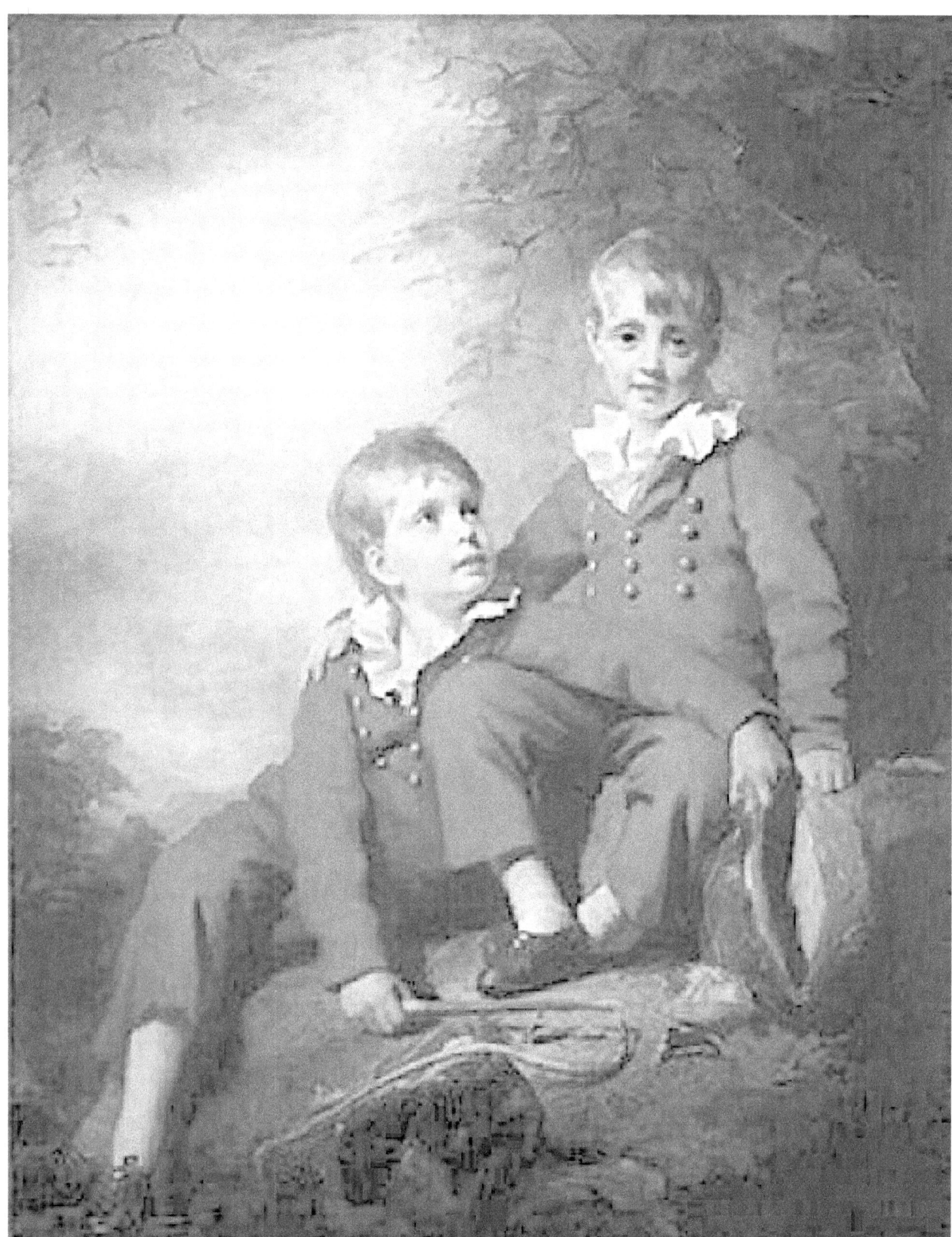

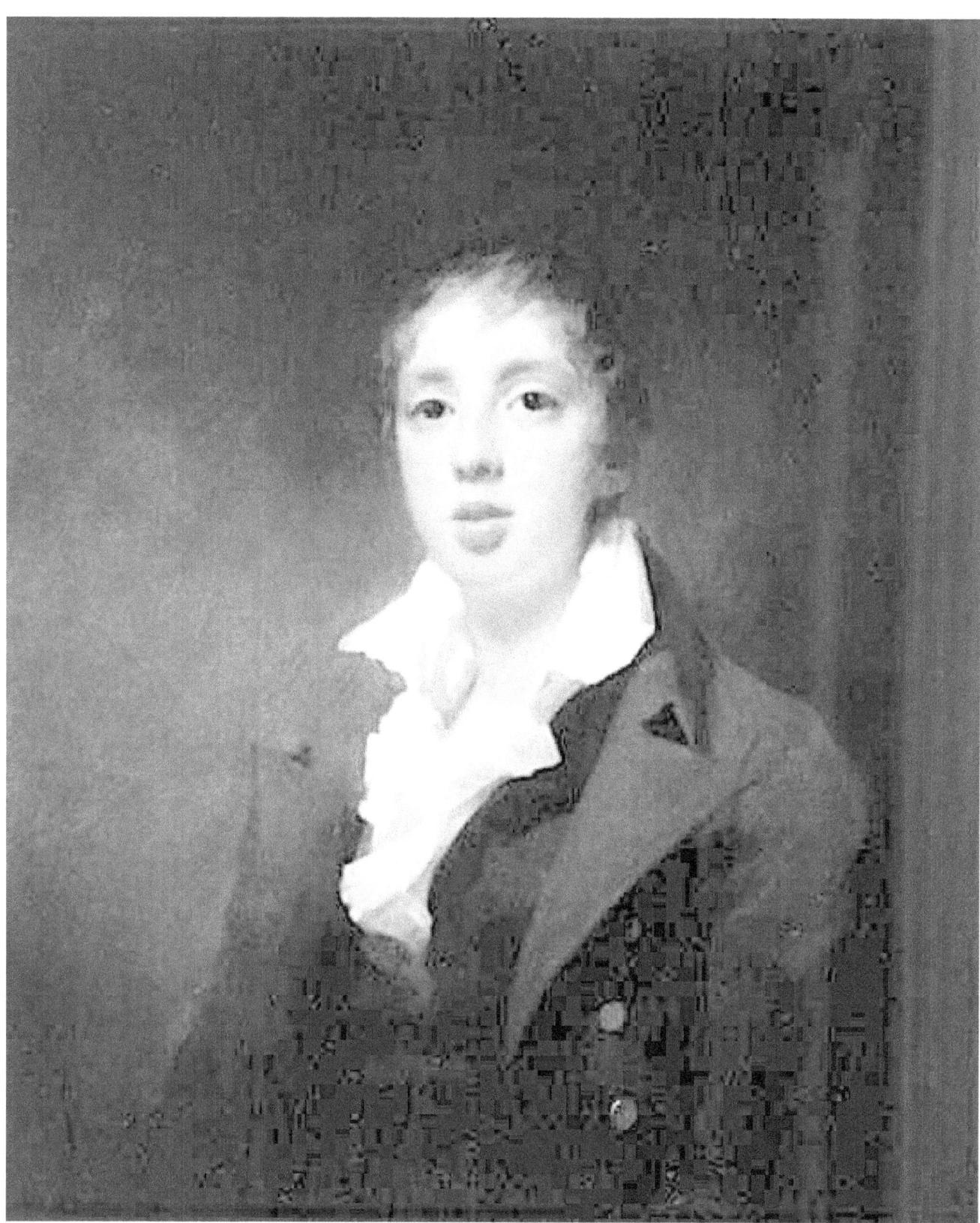

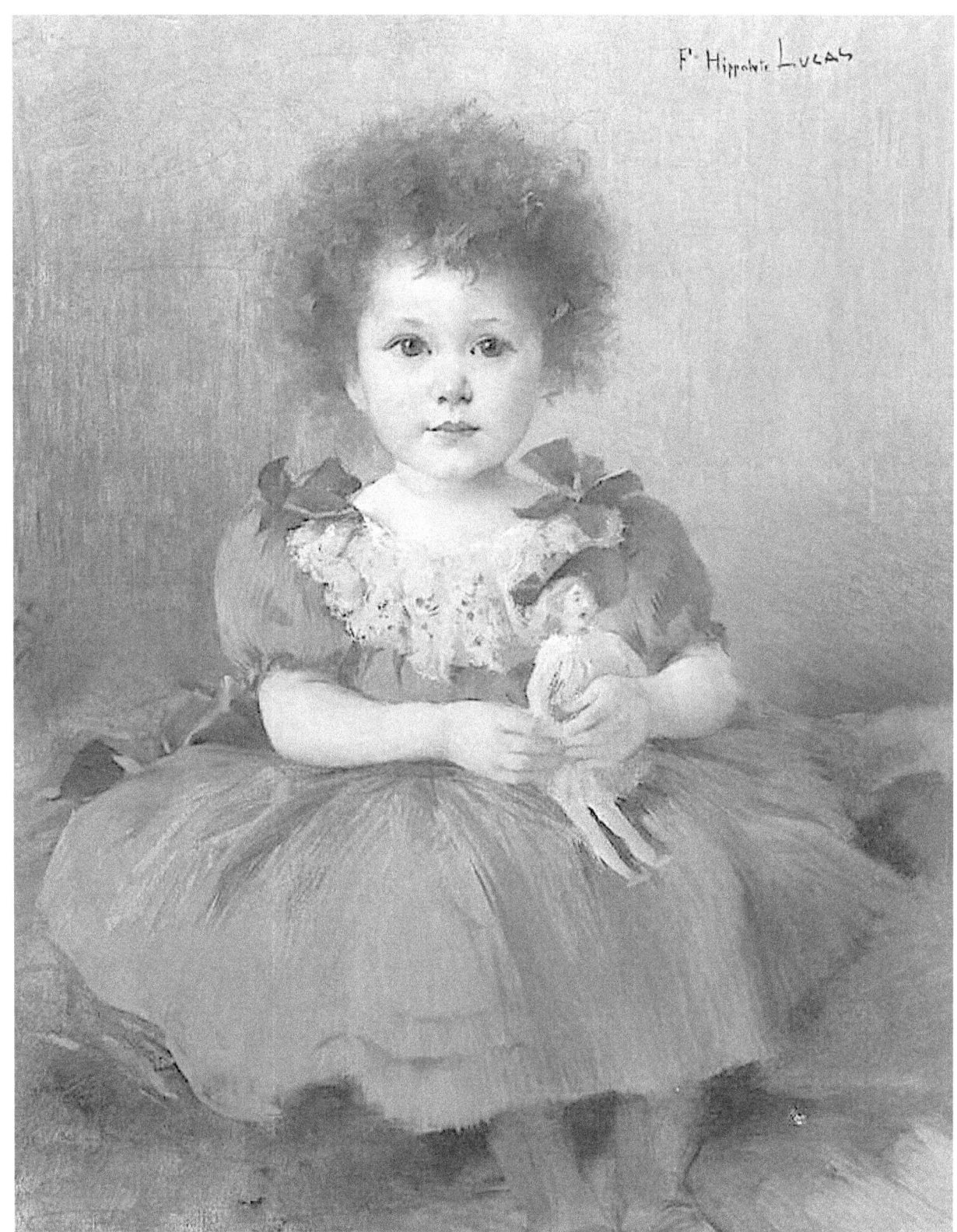

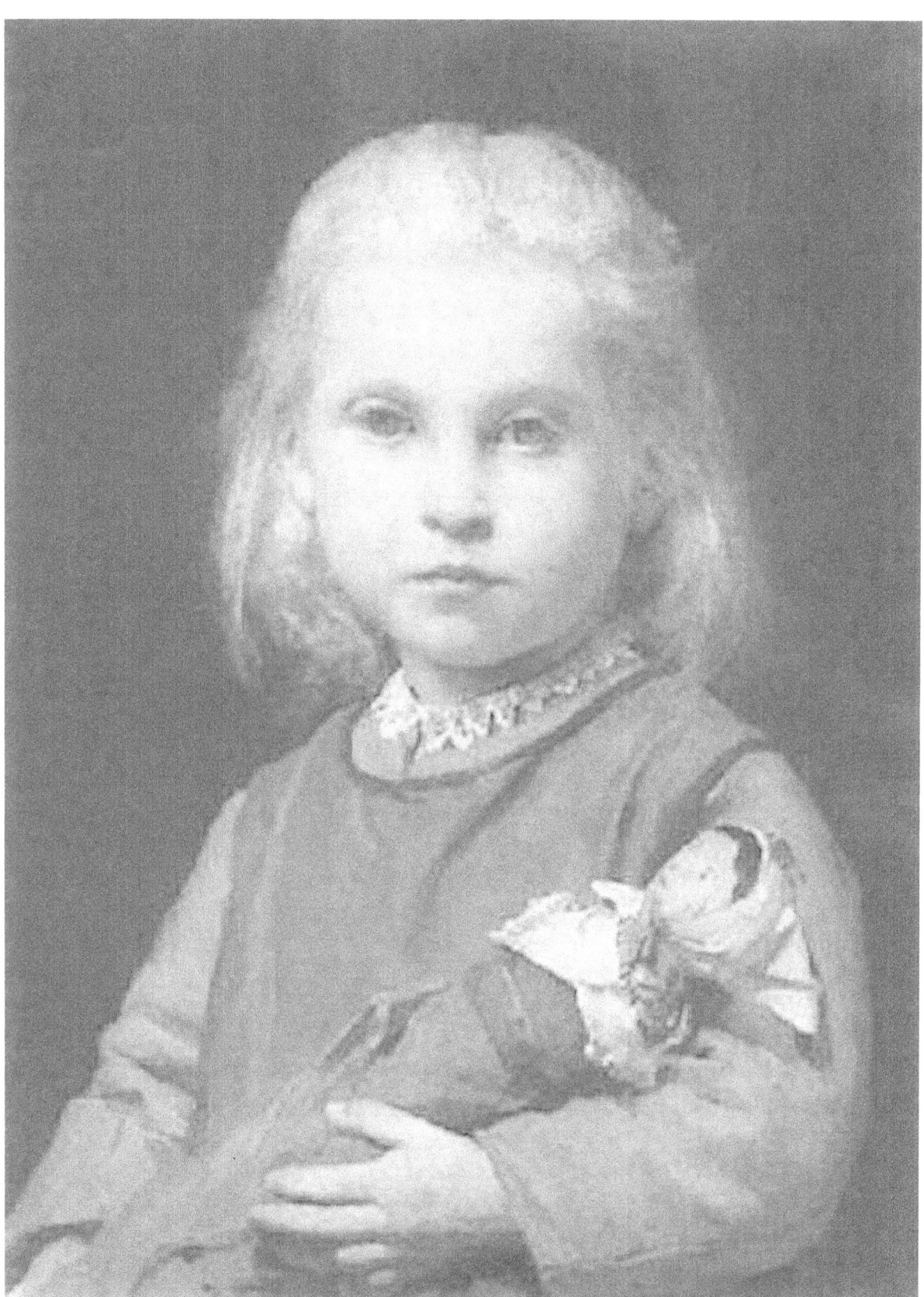

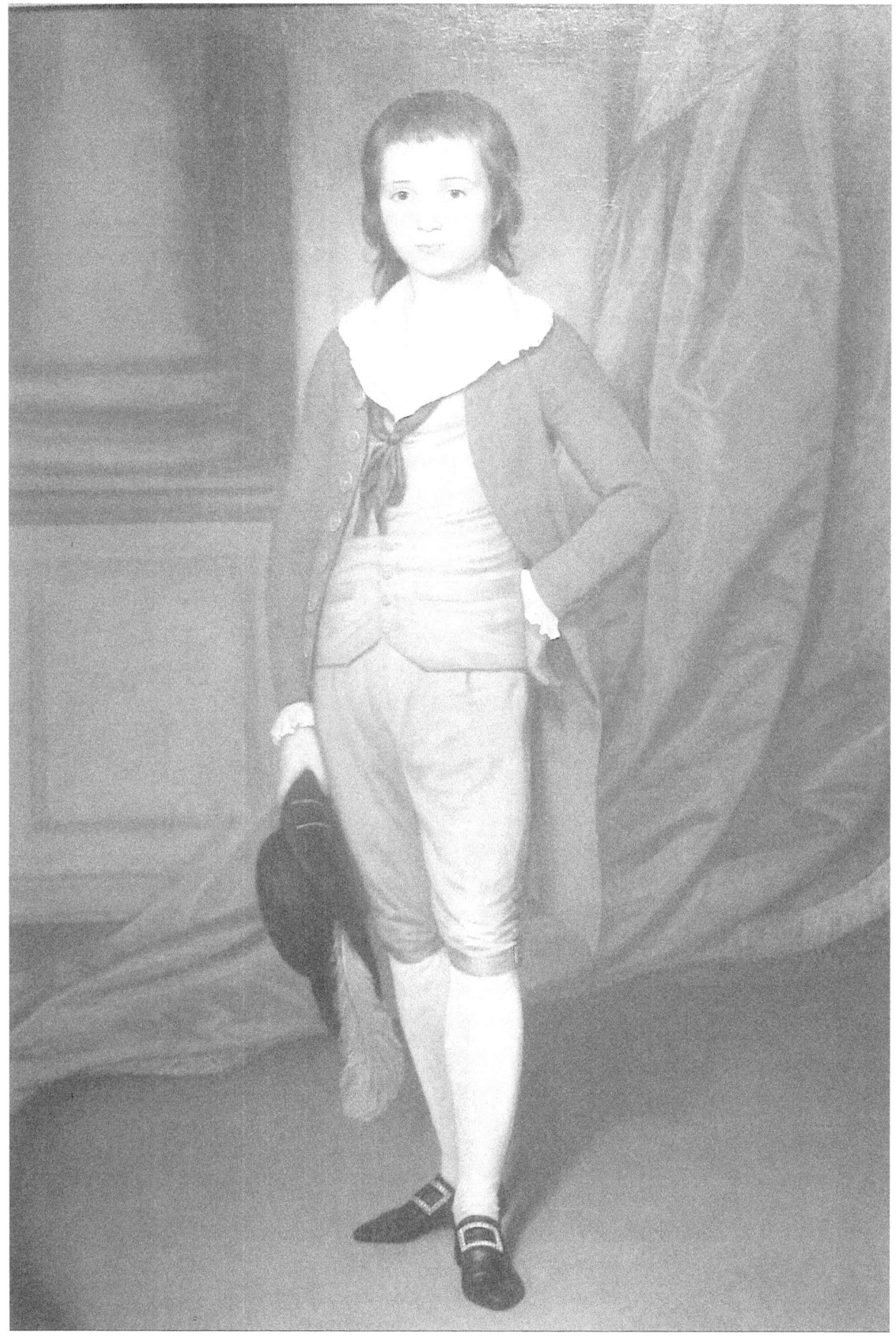

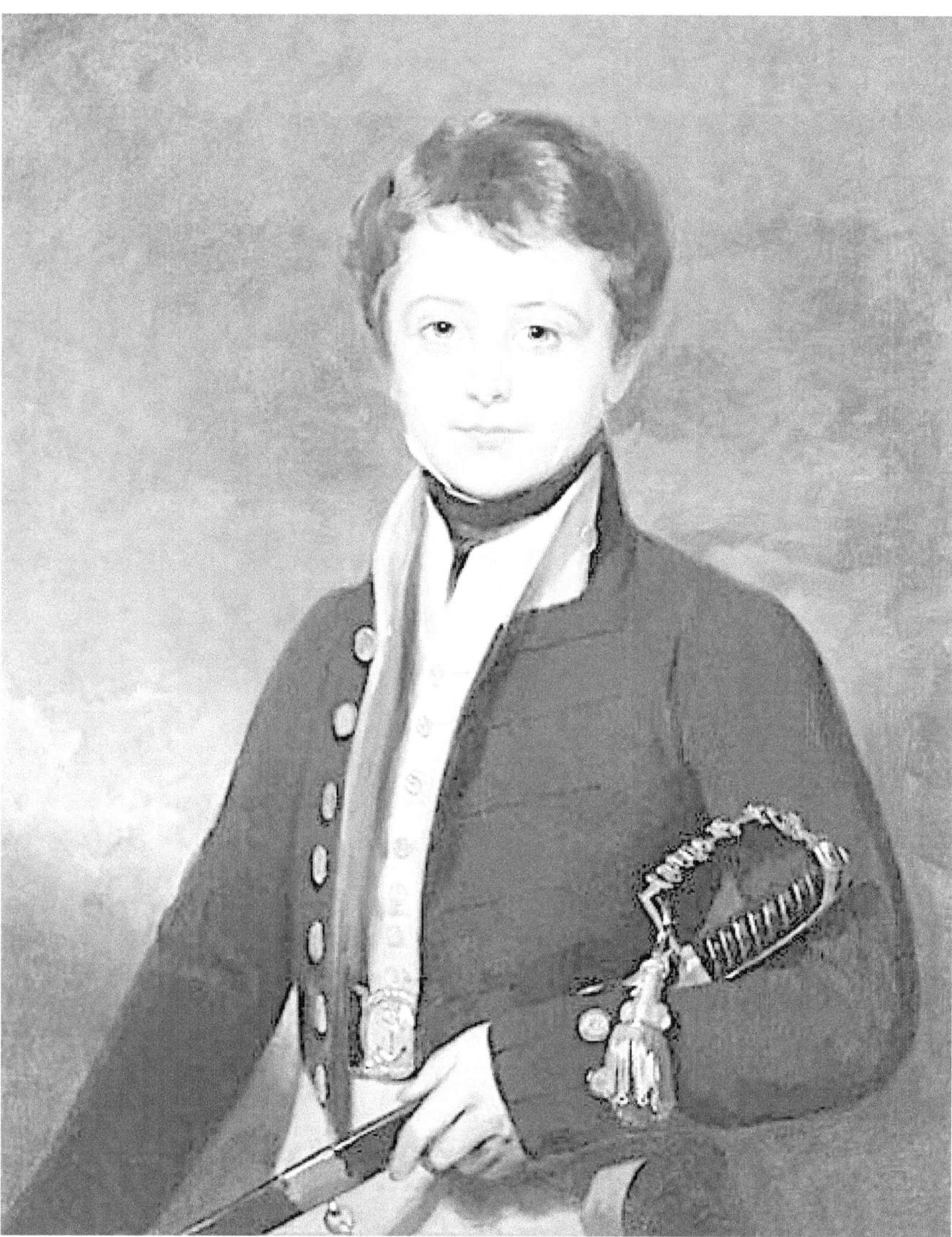

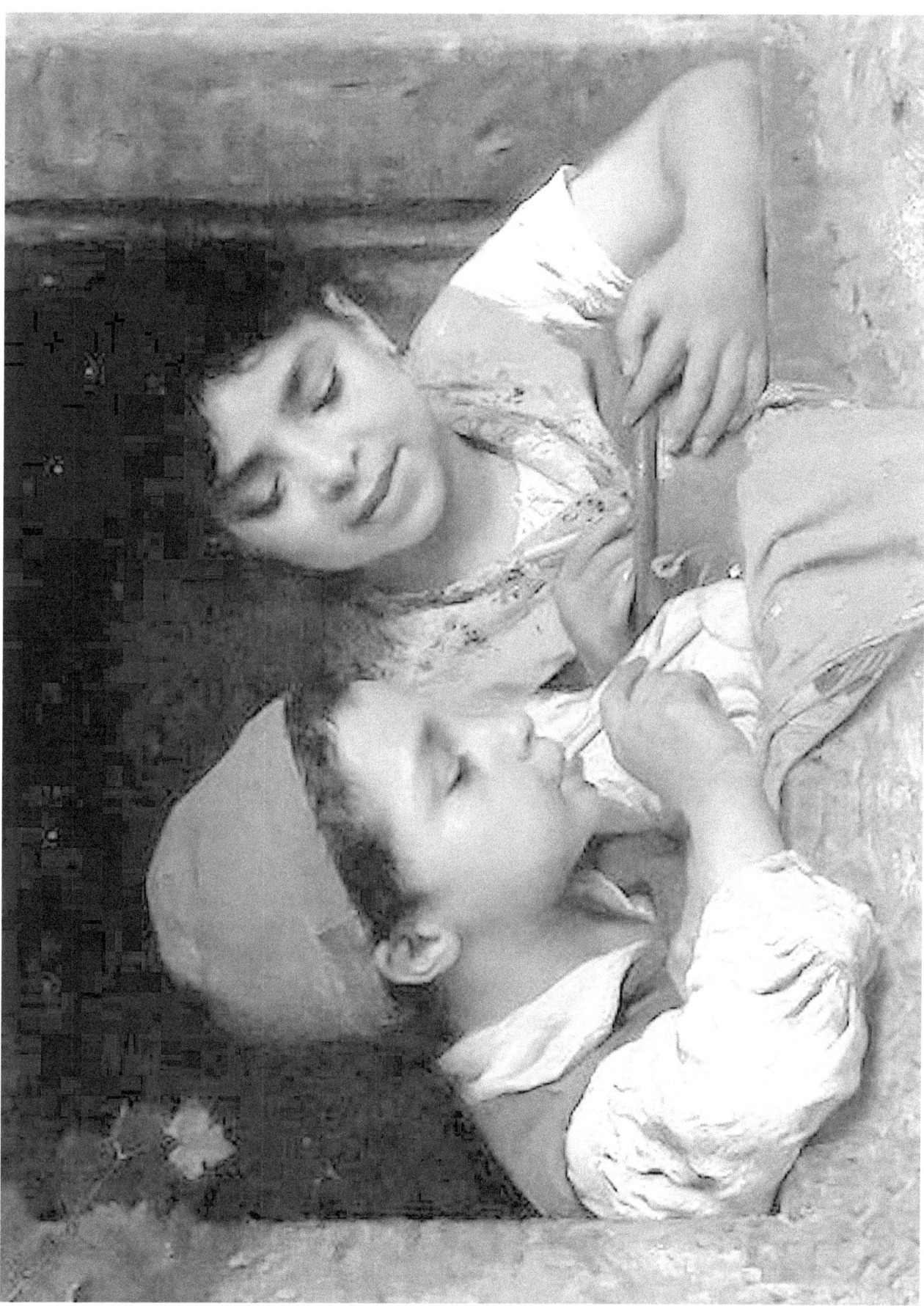

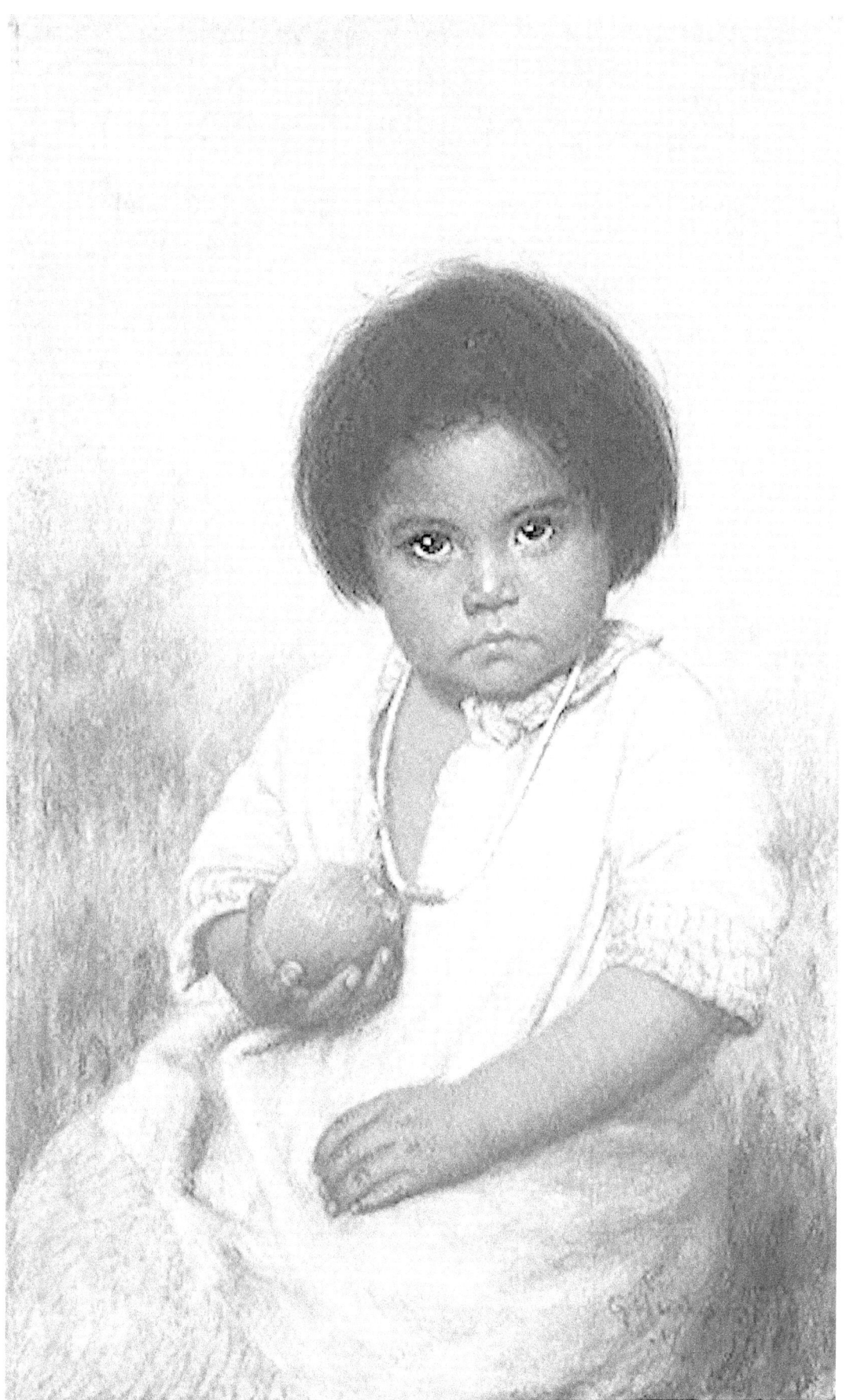

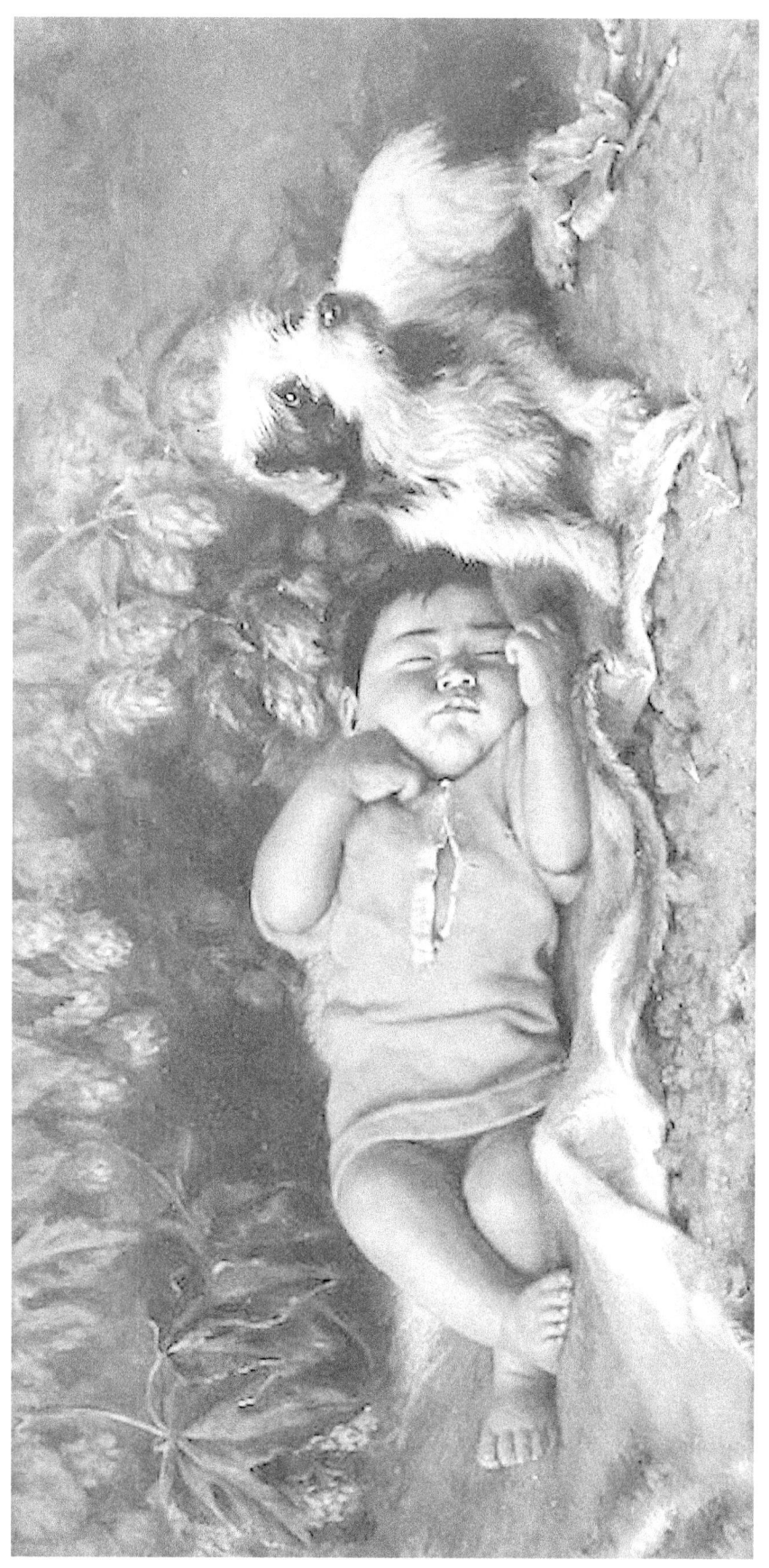

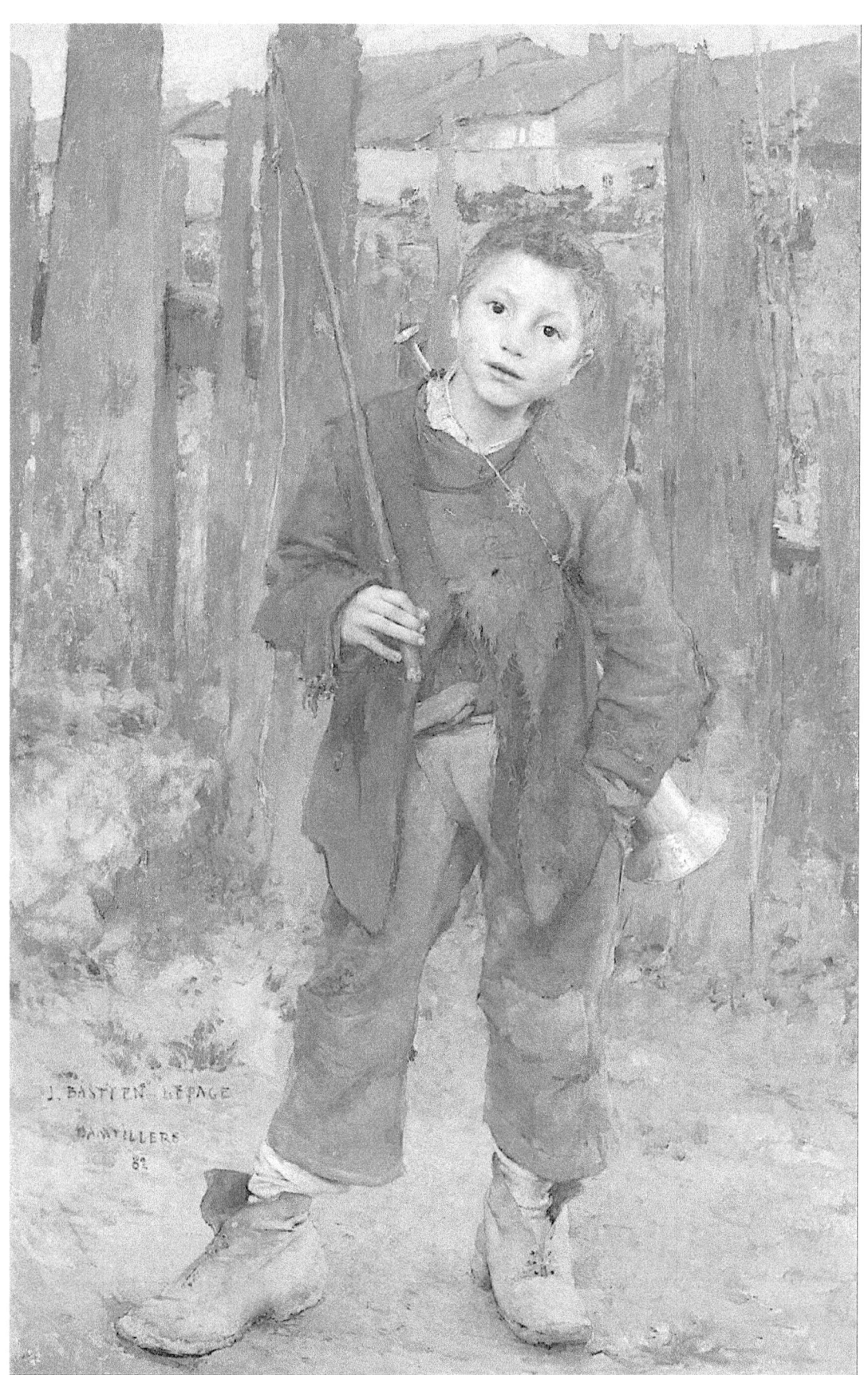

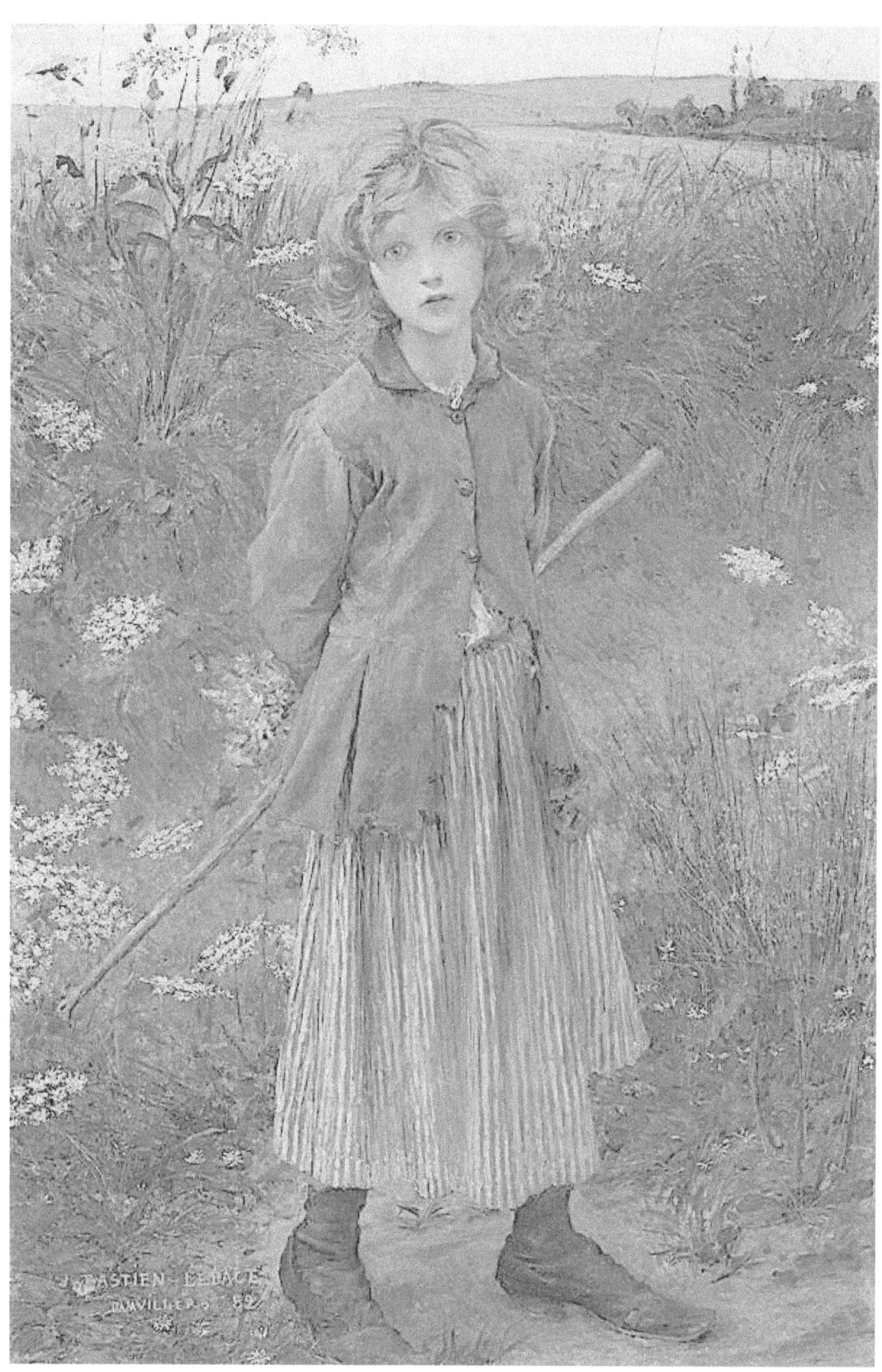

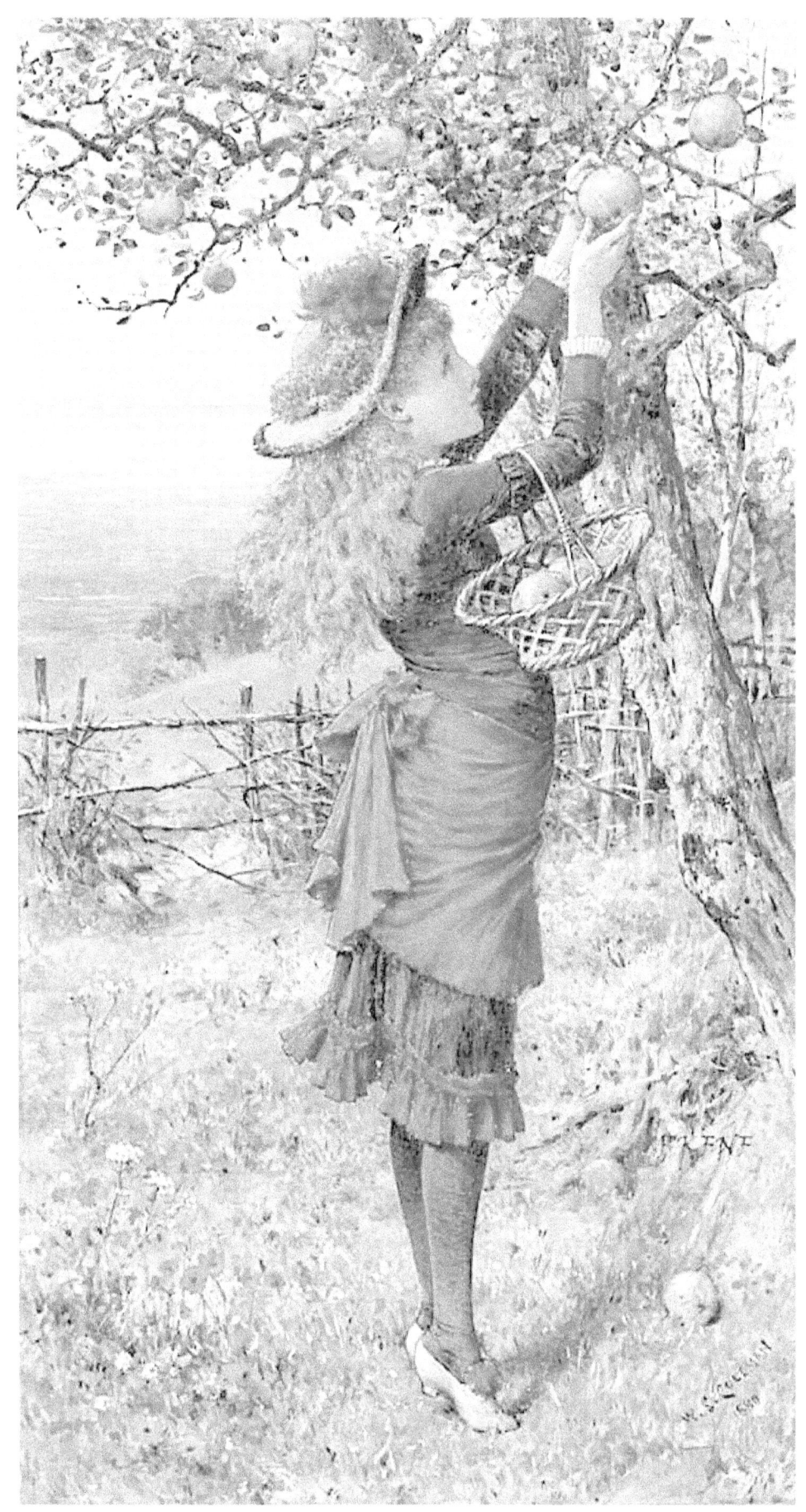

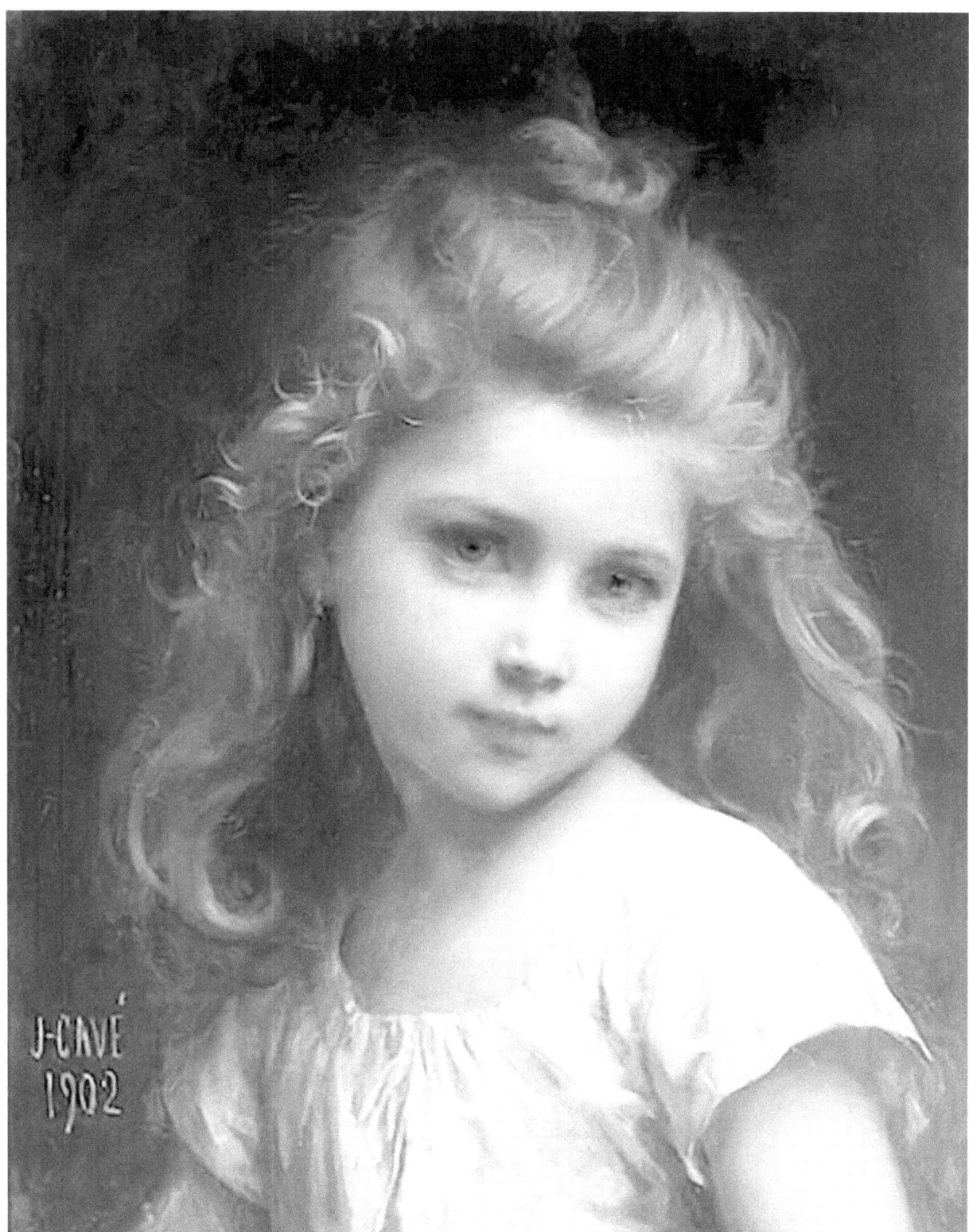

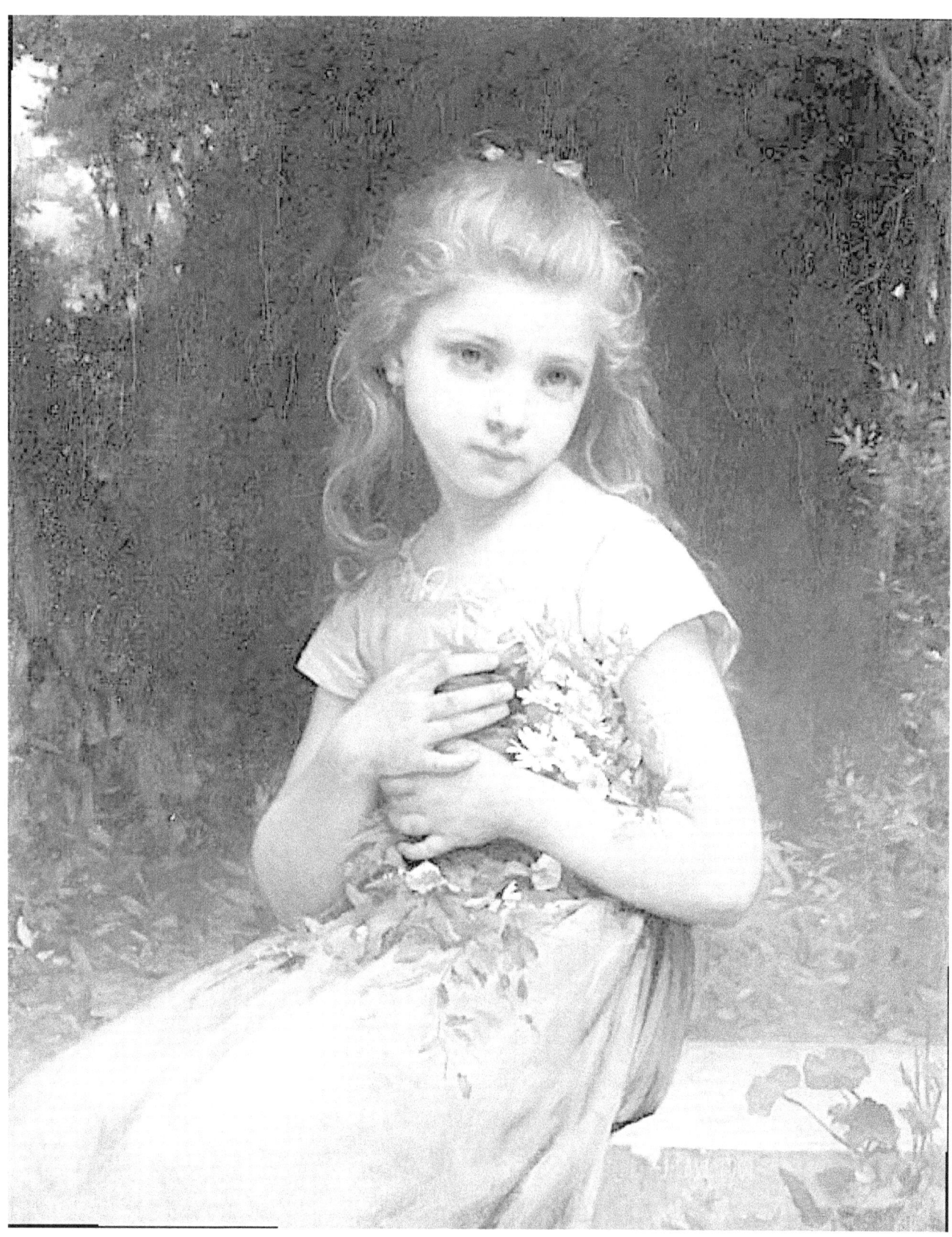

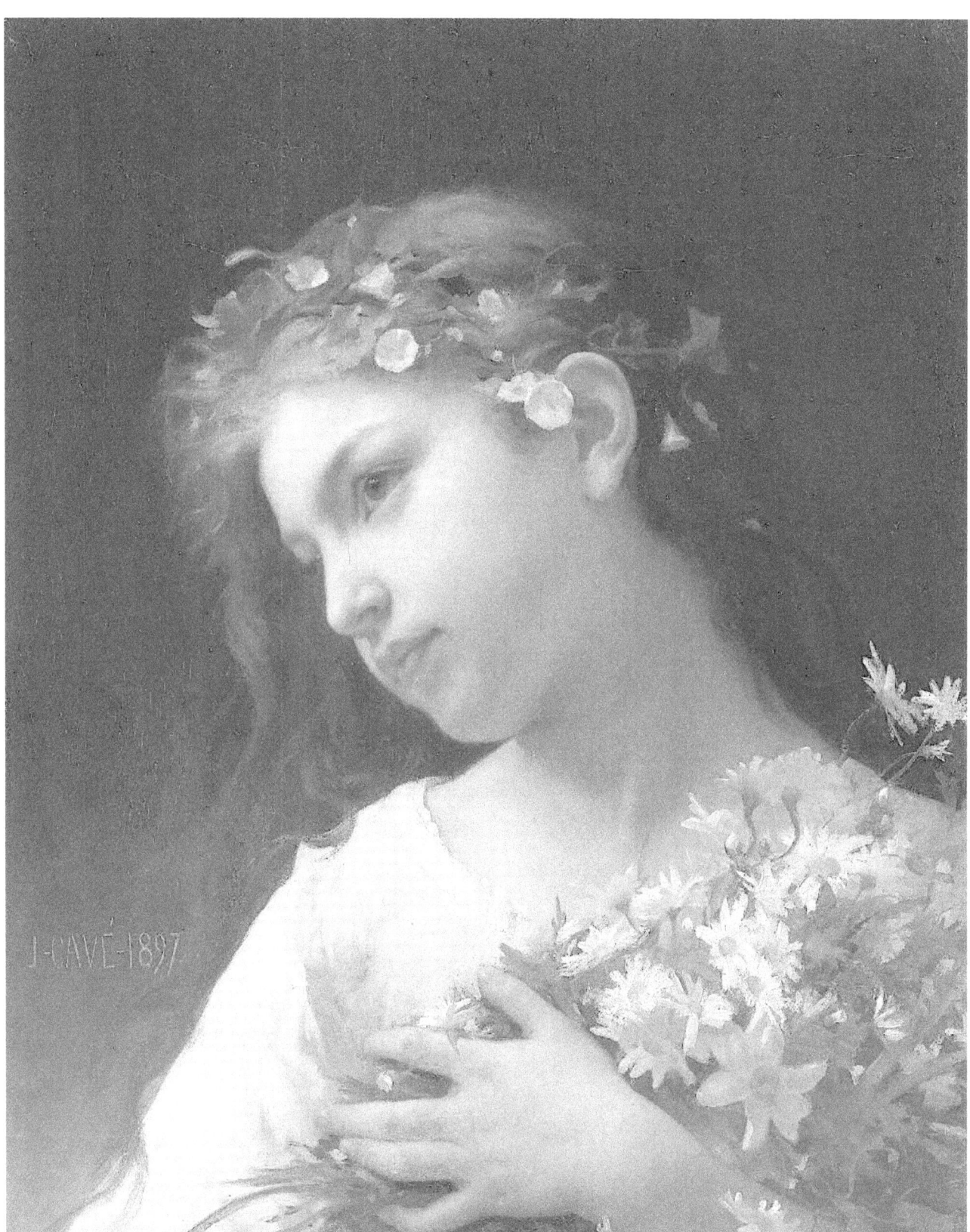

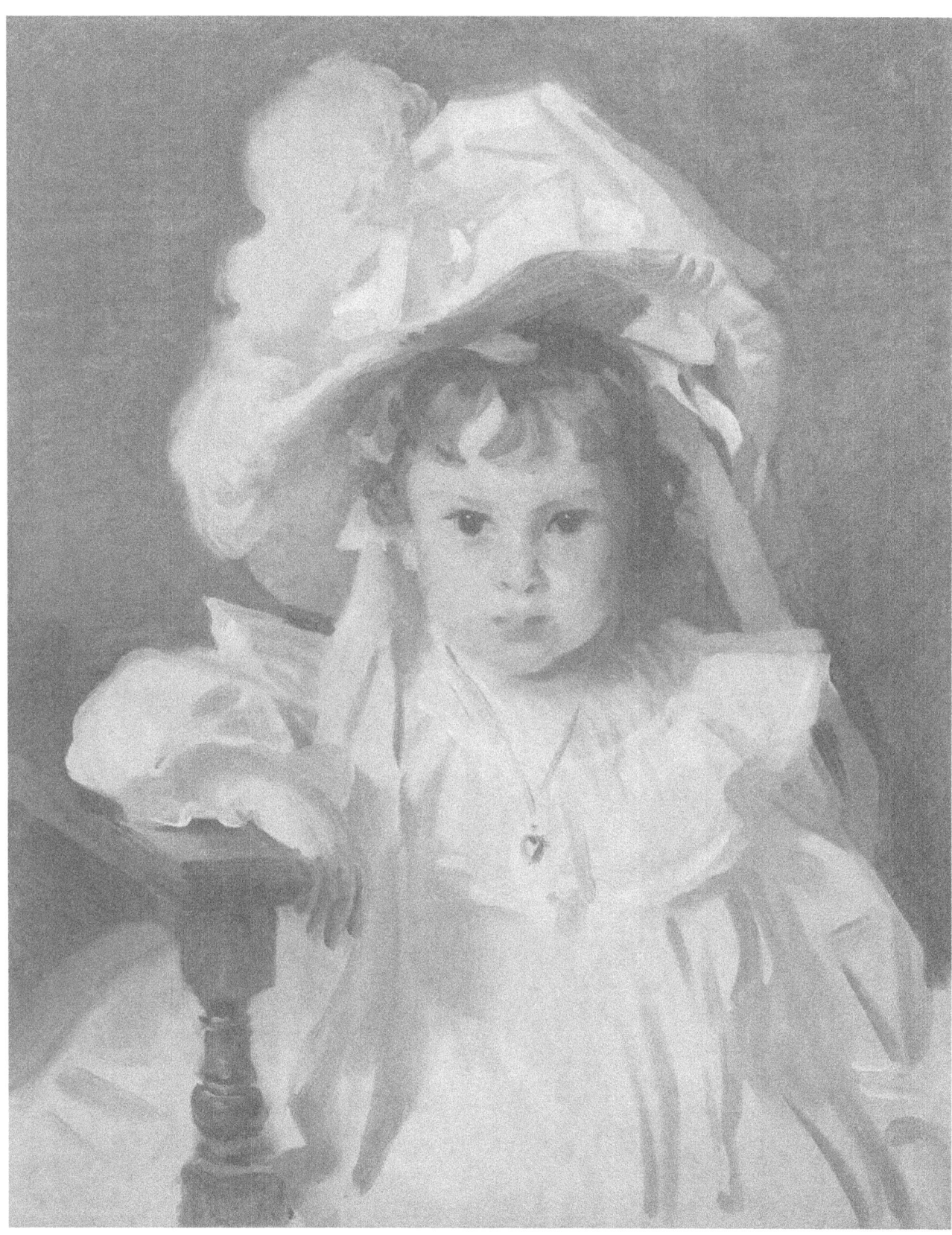

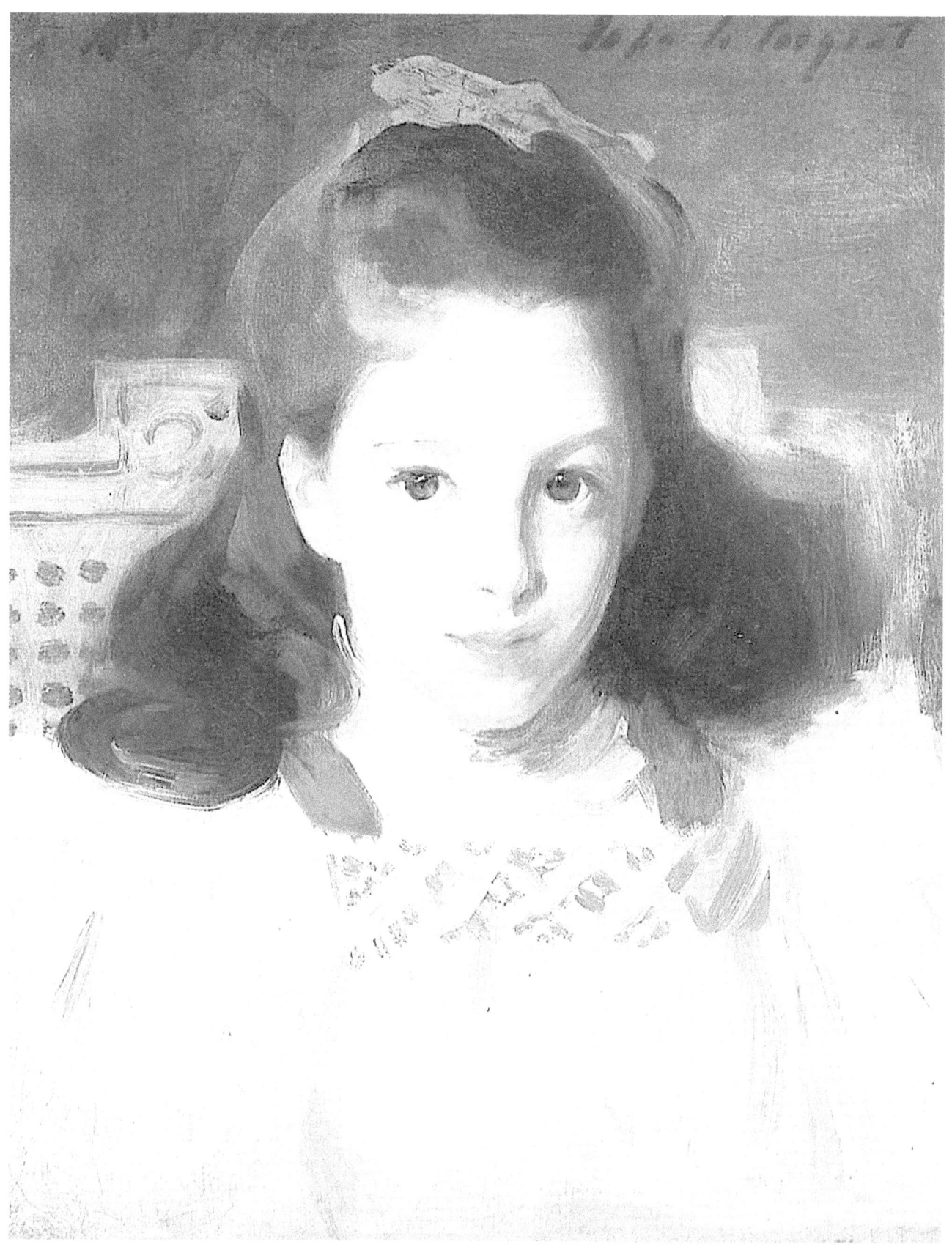

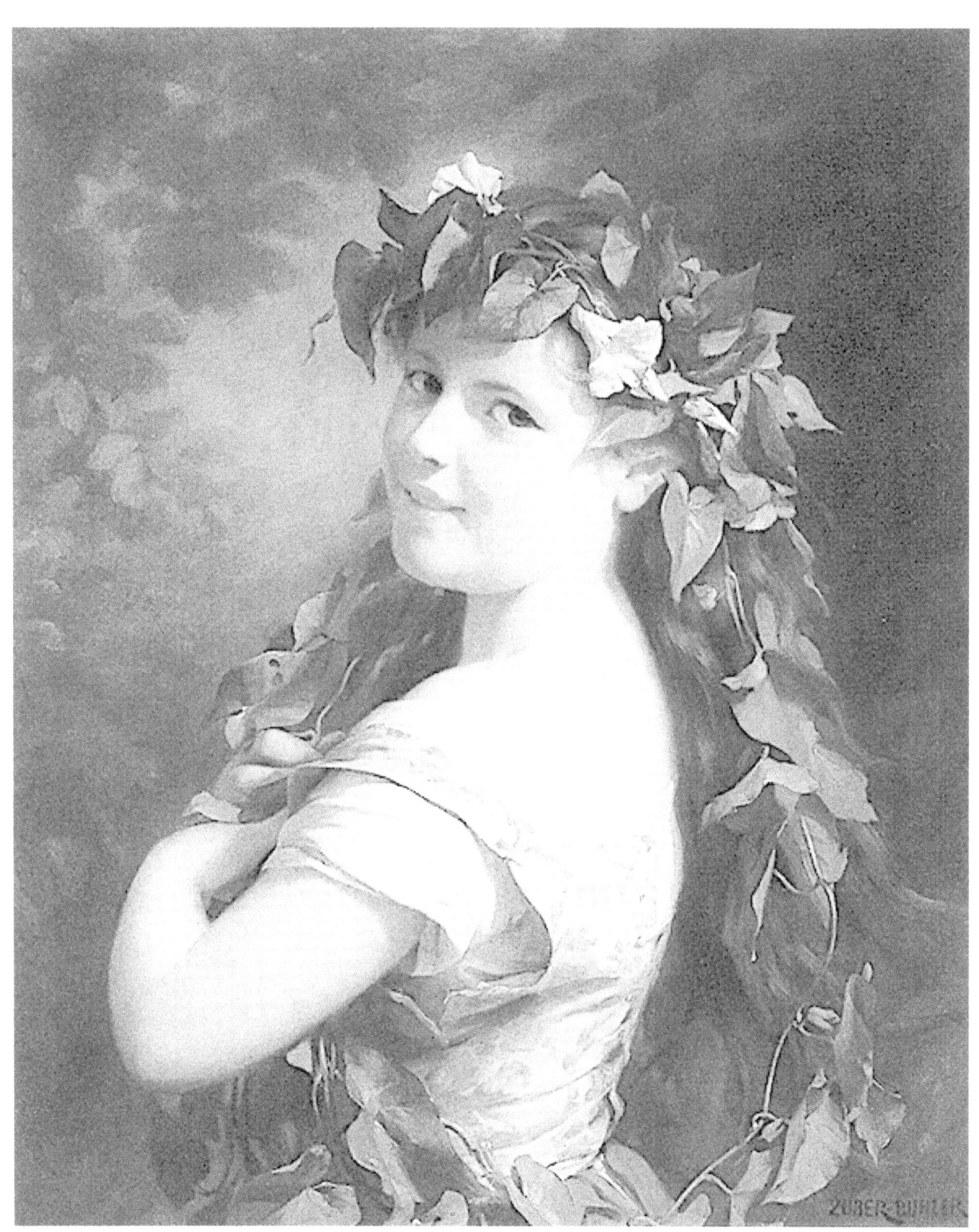

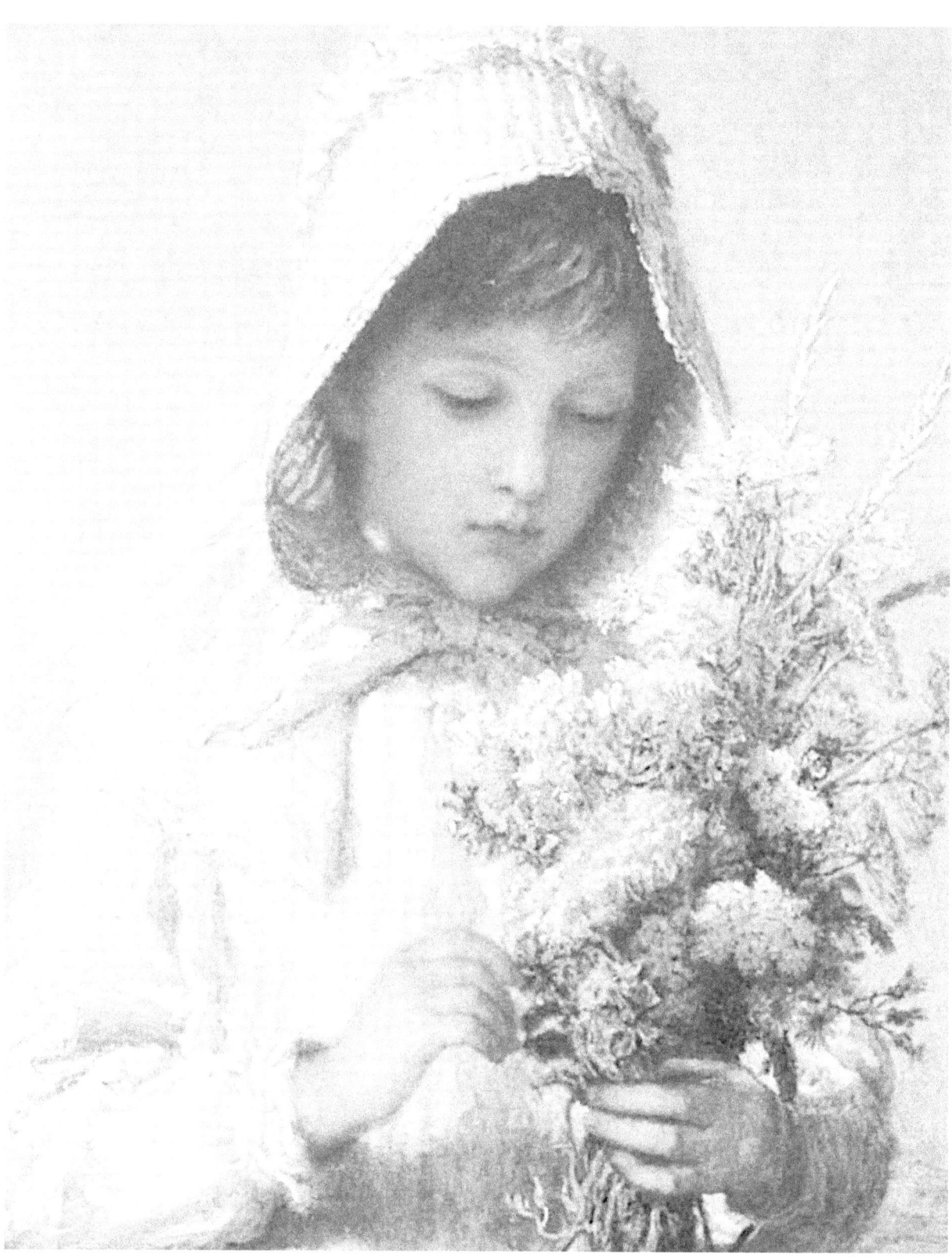

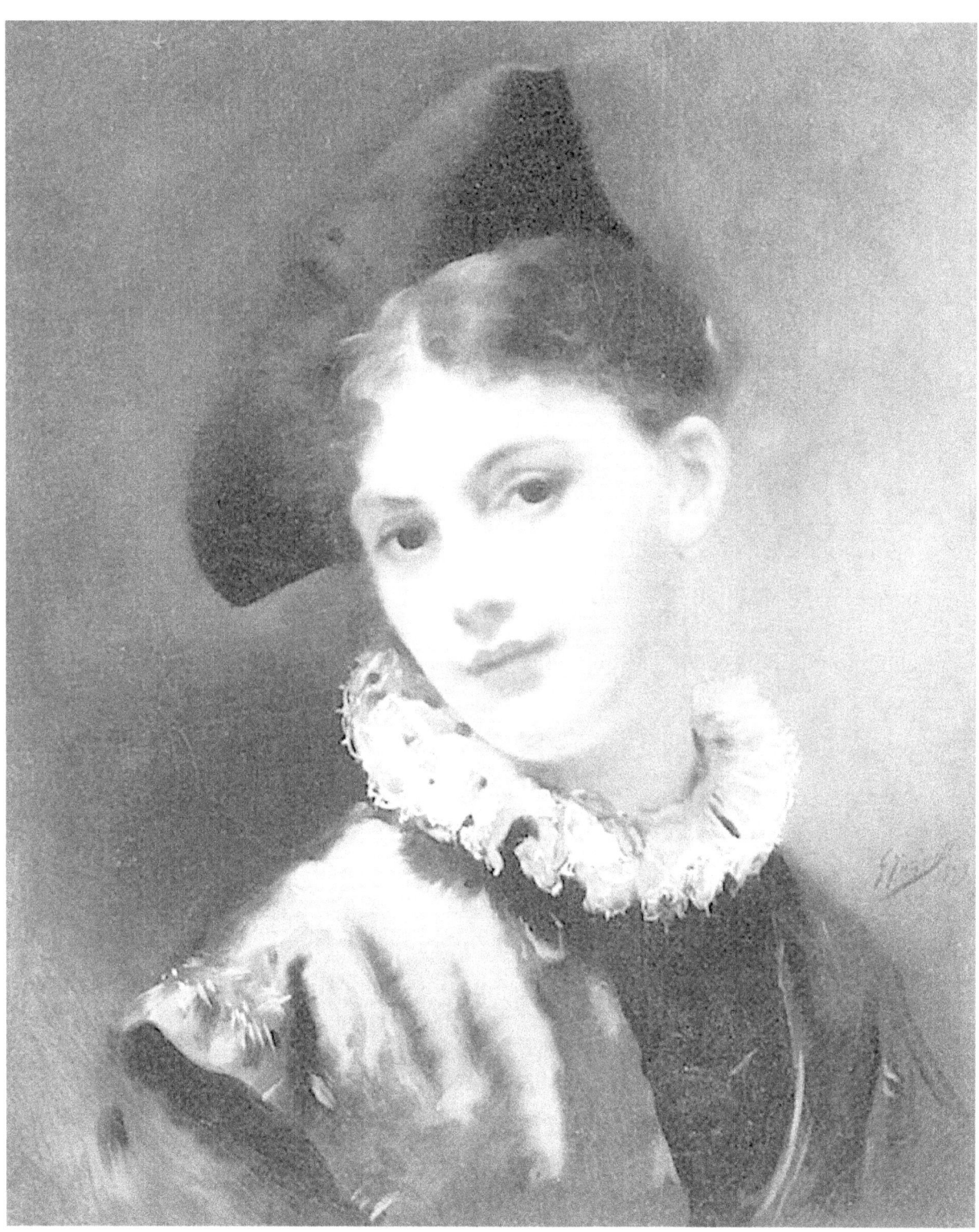

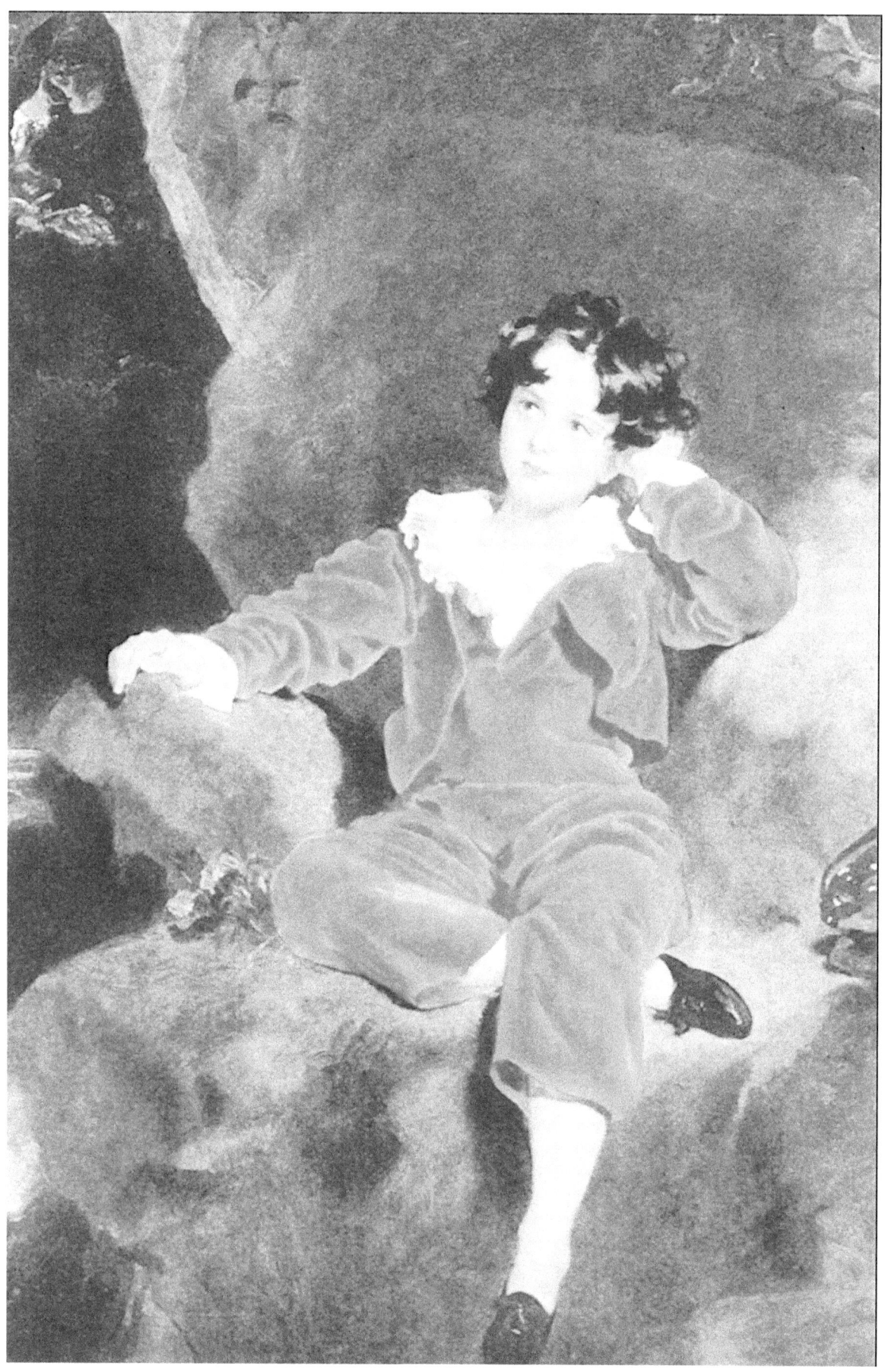

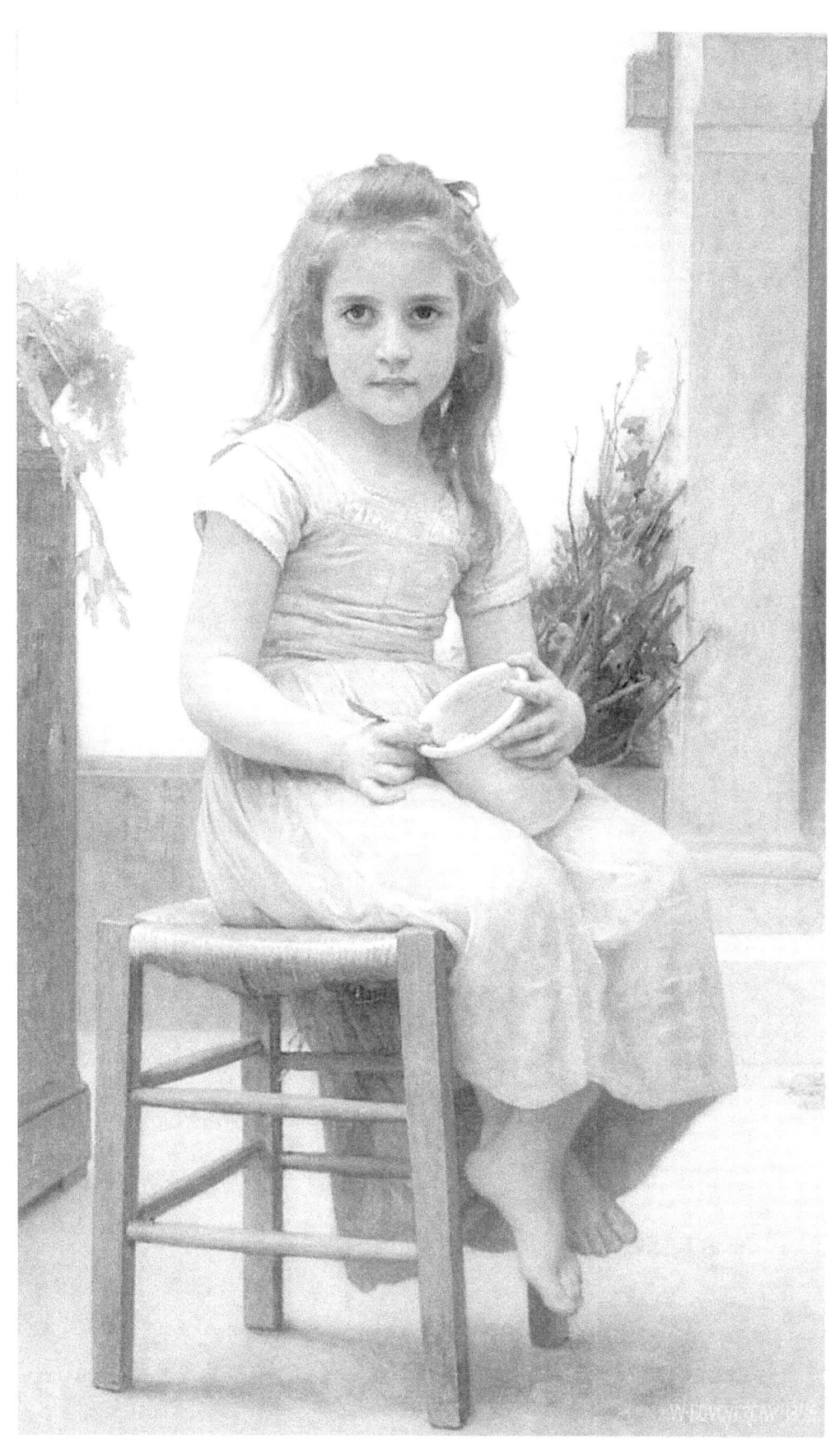

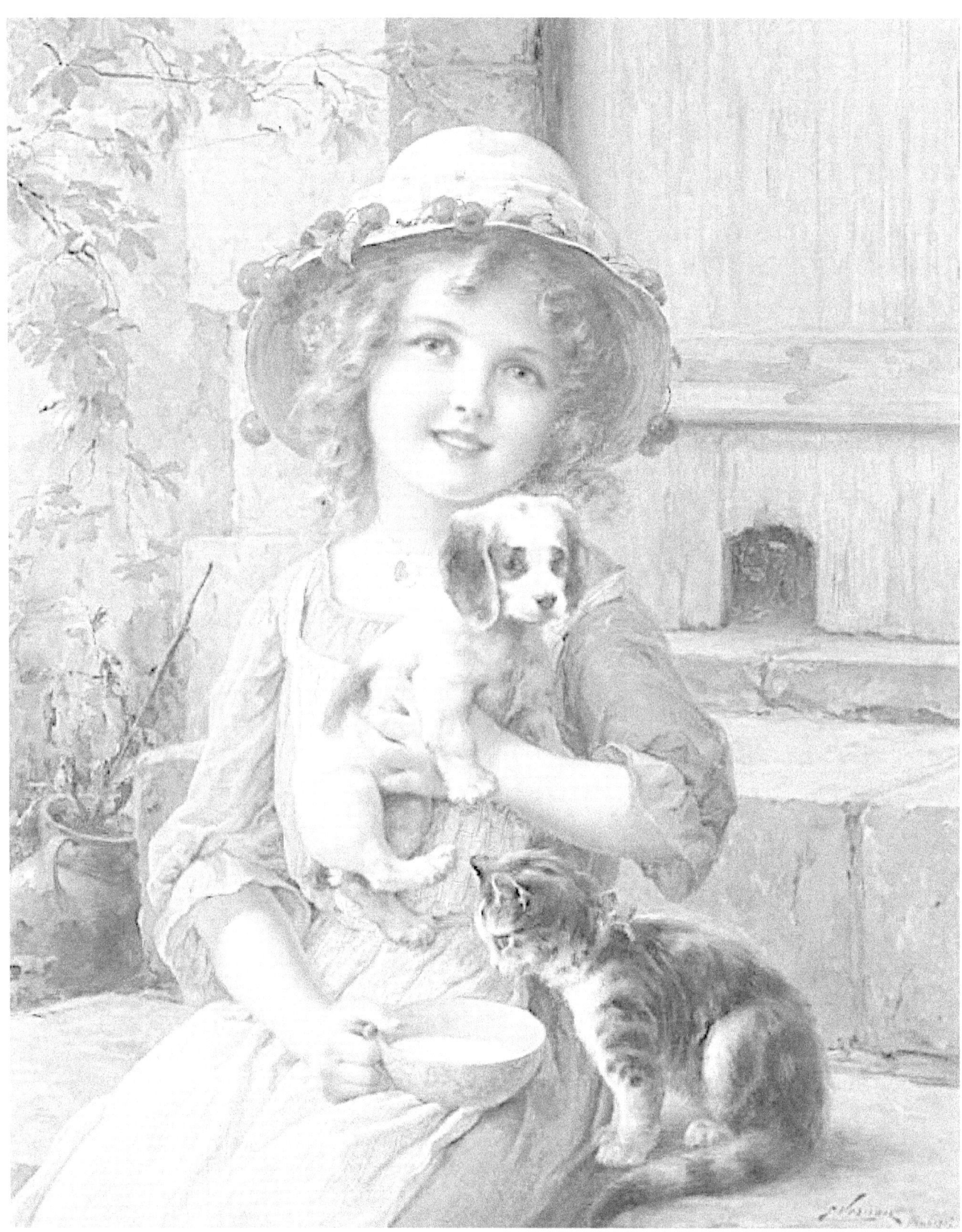

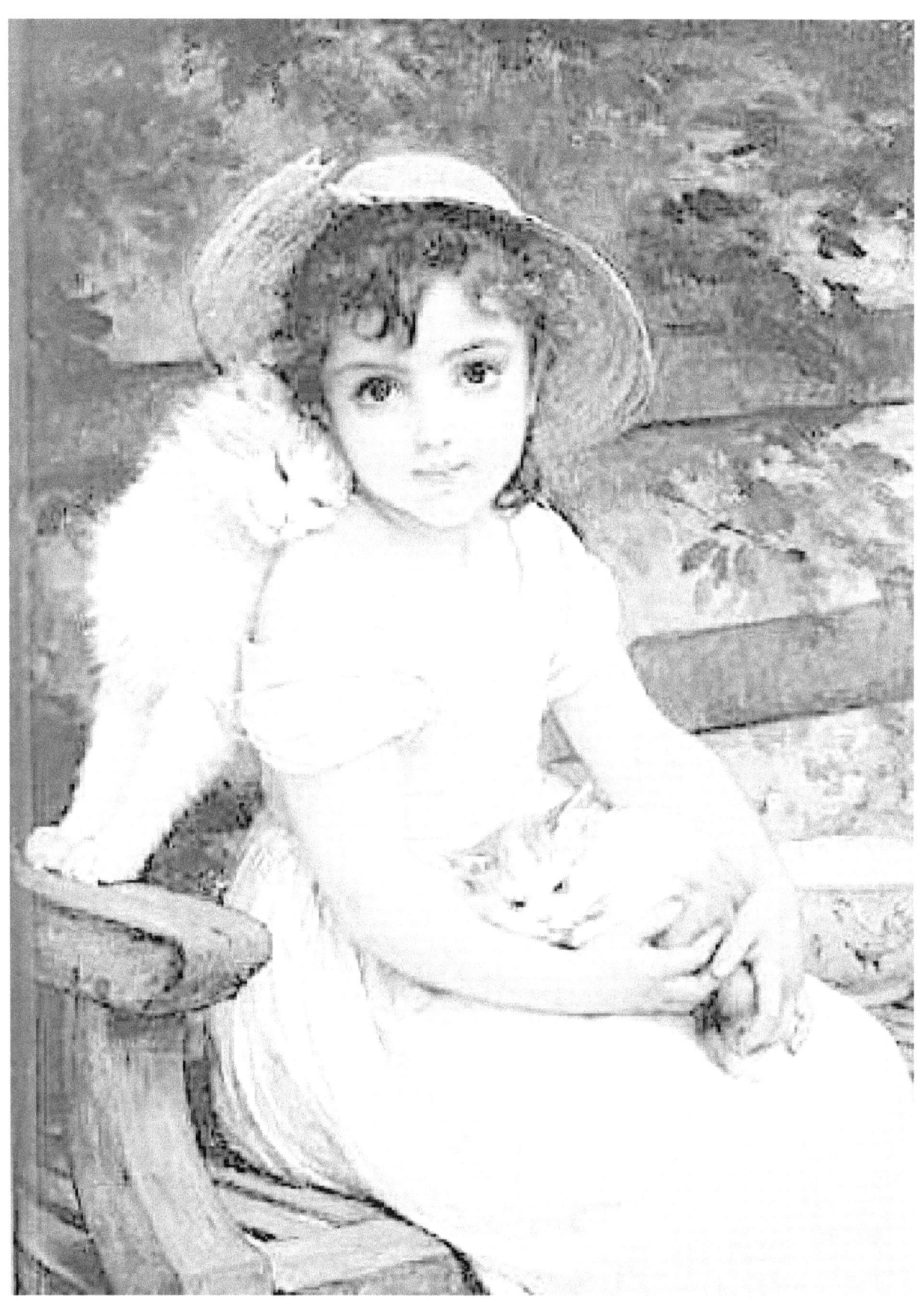

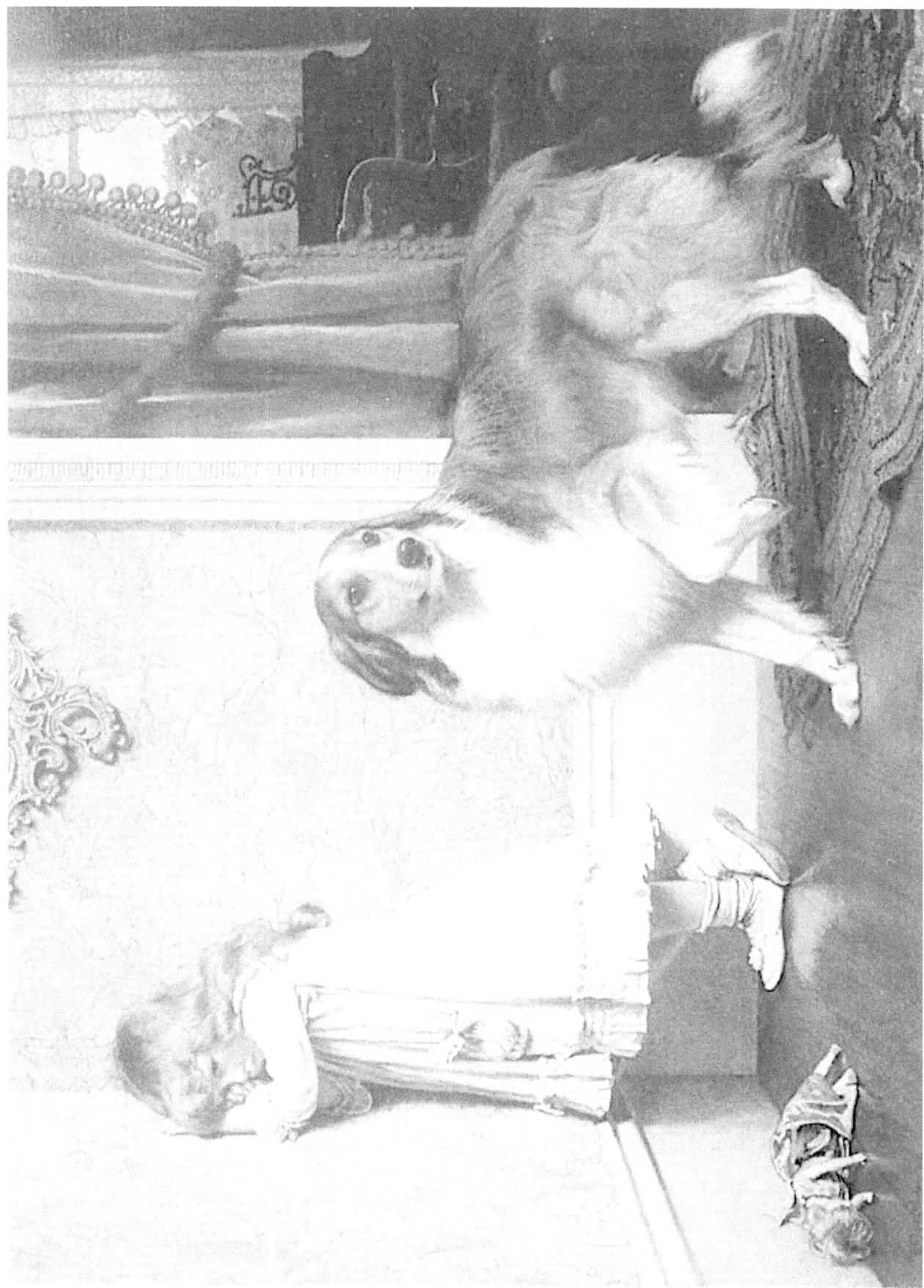

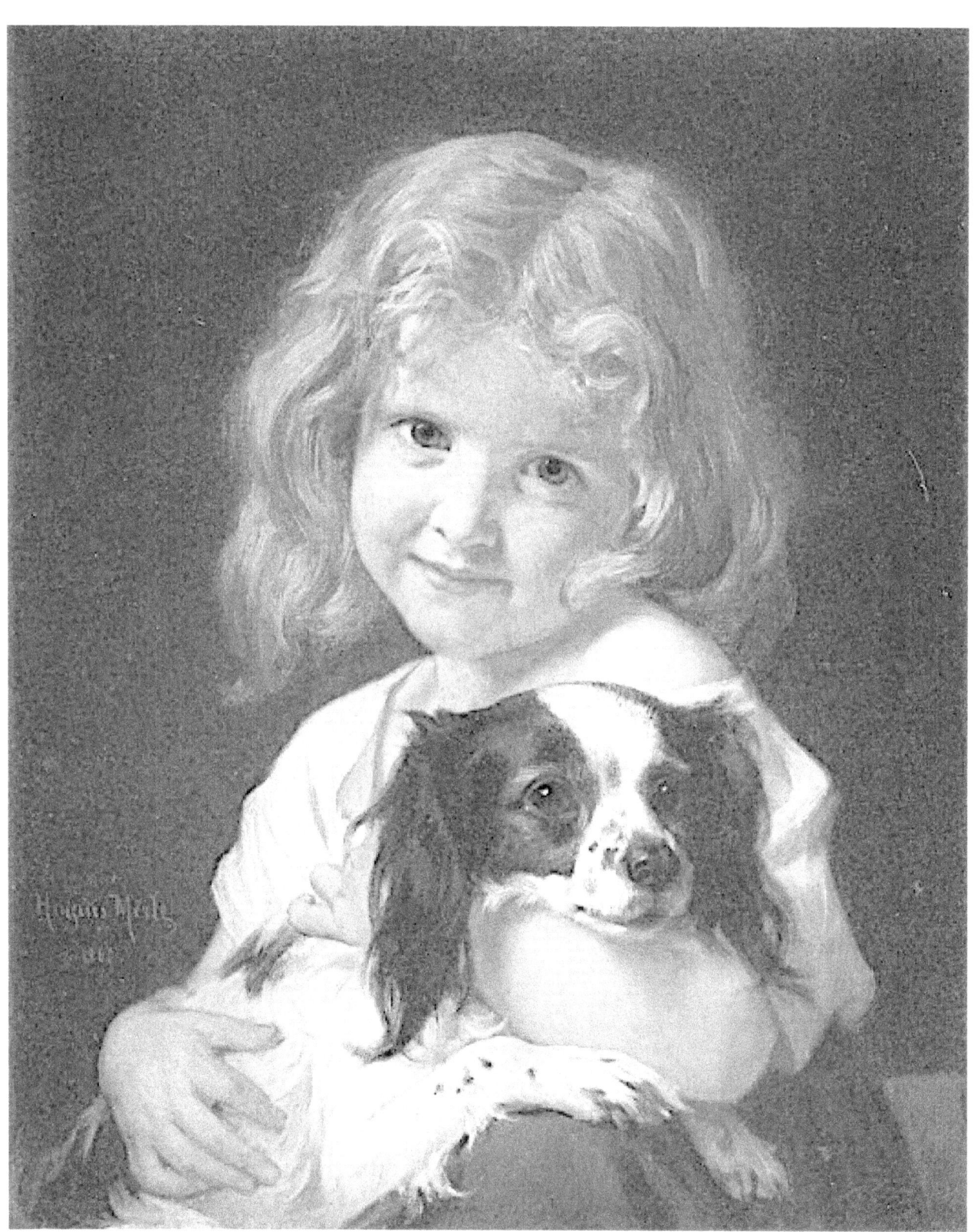

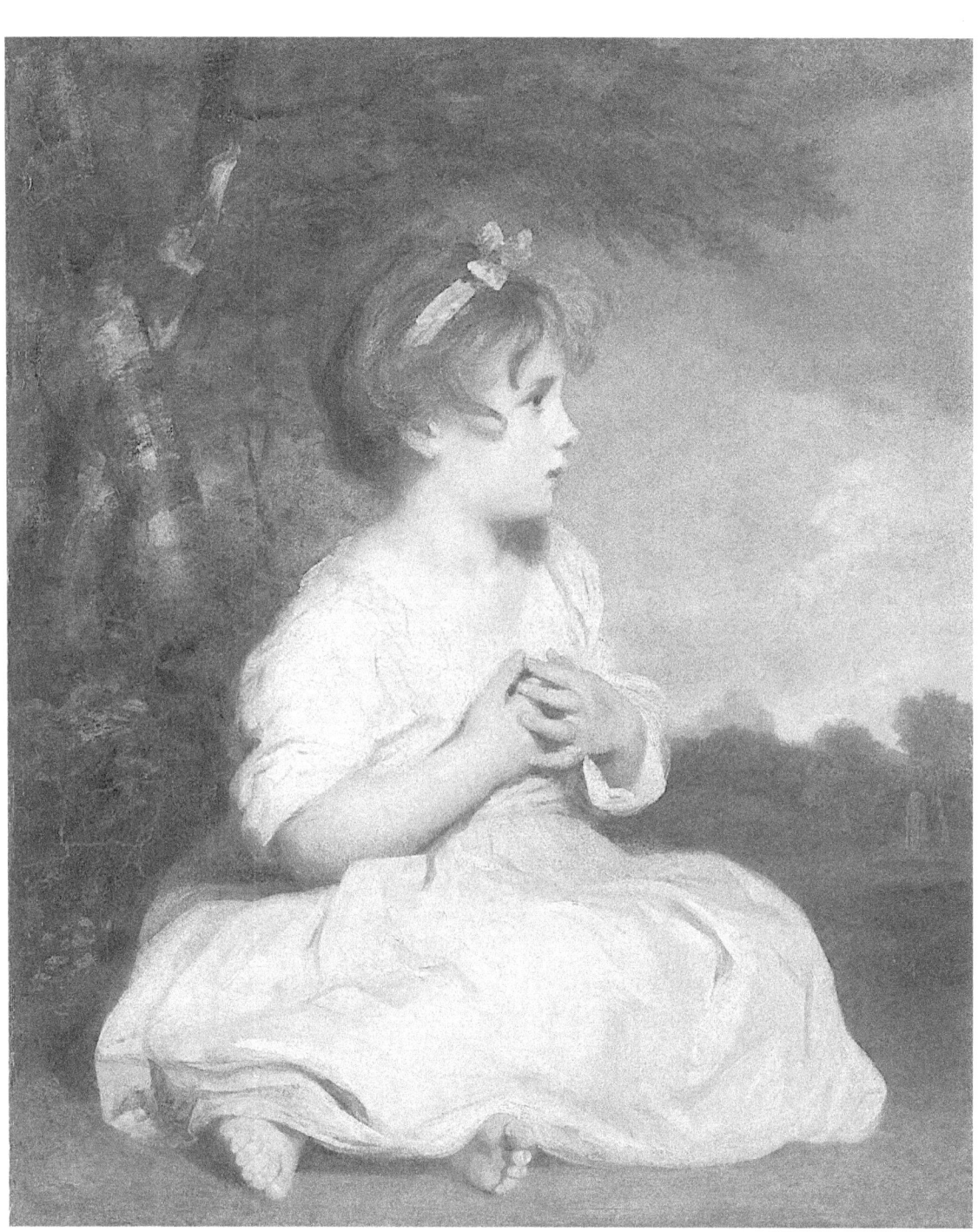

Each of these paintings is in the Public Domain. Here is the list of Vintage Paintings of Children in this grayscale coloring book.

1. Walter Firle, German, 1859-1929. Three Girls Reading a Fairytale (1890)

2. William-Adolphe Bouguereau, French.1825-1905 , oil on canvas. Deux Soeurs

3. Buhler Fritz Zuber, Swiss. 1822-1896. Oil on canvas. girl holding peonies

4. Buhler Fritz Zuber, Swiss. 1822-1896. Oil on canvas girl seated holding doll

5. Timoleon Marie Lobrichon, French. 1831-1914. Oil on canvas. Les Enfants Endormis

6. Charles Burton Barber, British. 1845-1894. Oil on canvas. Suspense

7. Heinrich Hirt 1841-1902- German - girl in long grass, skirt

8. Edouard Cabane, French, 1857-1942. painting - Jeune fille a la robe verte

9. German School, 18th Century. Portrait of a young man, said to be Prince Friedrich Hermann Otto von Hohenzollern-Hechingen. The Prince was born in 1717 died in 1838,

10. Gad Frederik Clement (9 July 1867 – 7 January 1933) Danish.-"Childrens Pastimes"

11. John Morgan, English. 1822-1865. Hide and Seek

12. Hendrikus van den Sande Bakhuyzen, Dutch. (1795-1860) - Contemplation

13. Hendrikus van den Sande Bakhuyzen, Dutch. (1795-1850) Dutch- Mary with her Teddy

14. Christen Brun, Norwegian 1828-1905. A Basket Of Ribbons. 1869.

15. Marianne Stokes 1855-1927 German, Portrait of a Boy with a Model Sailing Boat. 1893

16. Marianne Stokes 1855-1927 Dreaming. 1875

17. Grace Carpenter Hudson 1865-1937 American - Indian child with tear

18. Grace Carpenter Hudson 1865-1937 American - Baby Bunting 1894

19. Leslie George Dunlap - Portrait of the Artists Daughter

20. John Singer Sargent, American expatriate.1856-1925. Oil on Canvas. Caspar Goodrich

21. William-Adolphe Bouguereau (1825-1905) - the little knitter 1882

22. Arthur John Elsley - (1860-1952) Little Bo Beep 1900

23. Jean-Honore Fragonard 1732-1806 - The reader.

24. William-Adolphe Bougeureau 1825-1905- child carrying flowers 1878

25. Thomas Gainsborough's (1727–1788) - The Blue Boy 1779

26. William-Adolphe Bouguereau, French.1825-1905 , oil on canvas. Girl with Grapes Vendangeuse [The Grape Picker]

27. William-Adolphe Bouguereau, French.1825-1905 , oil on canvas. La lecon difficile 1884

28. William-Adolphe Bouguereau, French.1825-1905 , oil on canvas. Little Girl with a Bouquet

29. Helen Thomas Dranga - Portrait of a Polynesian Girl

30. Henry Raeburn (1756 – 1823, Scottish) The Allen Brothers

31. Henry Raeburn (1756 – 1823, Scottish) William Blair

32. Henry Raeburn (1756 – 1823, Scottish) The Binning Children

33. Henry Raeburn (1756 – 1823, Scottish) Portrait of Master John Fraser Reeling

34. Marie-Félix Hippolyte-Lucas (1854-1925) — Little Girl at the Rag Doll

35. Albert Anker (1831-1910) Swiss Little Girl with doll

36. Joseph Wright 1734-1797 John Coats Browne 1784

37. Sir Martin Arthur Shee, Irish, 1769-1850, Portrait of a Midshipman

38. Jean-Étienne Liotard 1702-1789- Children blowing bubbles by window

39. Grace Carpenter Hudson 1865-1937 American, Ray of Light (Da-Ta-Leu)

40. Grace Carpenter Hudson 1865-1937 American, Sleeping baby and dog

41. Jules Bastien-Lepage (1848–1884), Pas Mèche (Nothing Doing) (1882)

42. Jules Bastien-Lepage (1848–1884), Roadside Flowers (The Little Shepherdess) (1882)

43. WILLIAM STEPHEN COLEMAN, British. 1829-1904. Picking Apples

44. Jules Cyrille Cave (1859-1940) French, Portrait of a Young Girl, 1902)

45. Jules Cyrille Cave (1859-1940) French, "My Daisies" 1901

46. Jules Cyrille Cave (1859-1940) French, Girl with Bouquest of Daisies

47. John Singer Sargent, American expatriate.1856-1925. Oil on Canvas, Dorothy 1900

48. John Singer Sargent, American expatriate.1856-1925. Oil on Canvas Portrait of Miss Dorothy Vickers 1884.

49. Buhler Fritz Zuber, Swiss. 1822-1896. Oil on canvas. Girl with wreath

50. Karl Wilhelm Friedrich Bauerle, German. 1831-1912. Oil on Canvas. The Month of September.

51. Gustave Jean Jacquet, French. 1846-1909. A Coquettish Smile

52. Sir Thomas Lawrence 1769-1830, English. Oil on Canvas, "Master Charles William Lambton," also known as "The Red Boy," 1825.

53. William-Adolphe Bouguereau, French.1825-1905 , oil on canvas. Le goûter, (The Snack) 1895

54. Emile Vernon, French (1872-1920). Oil on canvas, "New Friends" (1917)

55. Émile Munier, French (1840-1895) "Best Friends"

56. Charles Burton Barber, British. 1845-1894. Oil on canvas. A Special Pleader

57. Hugues Merle (1822-1881) French. Best Friends.

58. Sir Joshua Reynolds, English. 1723-1792. A little girl.

www.ingramcontent.com/pod-product-compliance
Lightning Source LLC
Chambersburg PA
CBHW081432220526
45466CB00008B/2353